Babylon
– tarot

GW01045602

About the Author

Active in the magical community for decades, Sandra Tabatha Cicero is a Senior Adept of the Hermetic Order of the Golden Dawn. Together with Chic Cicero she has several books on the Golden Dawn in print with Llewellyn. She was born in Soldiers Grove, Wisconsin. She graduated from the University of Wisconsin, Milwaukee, with a bachelor's degree in the fine arts.

To Write to the Author

If you wish to contact the author or would like more information about this book, please write to the author in care of Llewellyn Worldwide and we will forward your request. Both the author and publisher appreciate hearing from you and learning of your enjoyment of this book and how it has helped you. Llewellyn Worldwide cannot guarantee that every letter written to the author can be answered, but all will be forwarded. Please write to:

Sandra Tabatha Cicero
⁒ Llewellyn Worldwide
2143 Wooddale Drive, Dept. 0-7387-0719-6
Woodbury, Minnesota 55125-2989, U.S.A.
Please enclose a self-addressed stamped envelope for reply,
or $1.00 to cover costs. If outside U.S.A., enclose
international postal reply coupon.

Many of Llewellyn's authors have websites with additional information and resources.
For more information, please visit our website at
http://www.llewellyn.com

Babylonian

- *tarot* -

Sandra Tabatha Cicero

Llewellyn Publications
Woodbury, Minnesota

First Edition
First Printing, 2006

Book design by Donna Burch
Cover art © 2005 by Sandra Tabatha Cicero
Cover design by Ellen Dahl

Llewellyn is a registered trademark of Llewellyn Worldwide, Ltd.

Library of Congress Cataloging-in-Publication Data (Pending)
ISBN 13: 978-0-7387-0716-7
ISBN 10: 0-7387-0716-3

Llewellyn Publications
A Division of Llewellyn Worldwide, Ltd.
2143 Wooddale Drive, Dept. 0-7387-0719-6
Woodbury, Minnesota 55125-2989, U.S.A.
www.llewellyn.com

Printed in the United States of America

Other Books by This Author

The Essential Golden Dawn

The Golden Dawn Magical Tarot

Golden Dawn Enochian Skrying Tarot

Self-Initiation into the Golden Dawn Tradition

Contents

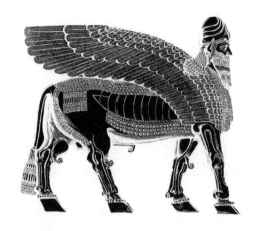

— Introduction —

Babylonian Tarot is based on the cosmology and legends of ancient Mesopotamia which is Greek for "the land between the rivers." Even older than mighty Egypt, Mesopotamia was the original cradle of civilization located in the Fertile Crescent valley between the Tigris and Euphrates rivers—an area now occupied by modern-day Iraq. Archeologists divide Mesopotamia into two sections: Lower Mesopotamia, which stretched from the river delta at the top of the Persian Gulf to what is now the city of Baghdad, and Upper Mesopotamia, which extended from Baghdad through Eastern Syria to the foothills of the Taurus Mountains in southeastern Turkey. It was in Mesopotamia, or *Babylonia* as it is often called, that the world's first cities appeared during the fourth millennium B.C.E.

The city of Babylon has long been the primary symbol for all of Mesopotamia. The Biblical stories suggest only negative connotations of the city—hardly an unbiased account. Ironically, many elements of Babylonian spiritual beliefs, practice, and mythos have found their way into the Hebrew Scriptures in such stories as the creation of the universe and the Great Flood. Fortunately recent archeological discoveries have given us a more accurate and balanced description of a vibrant and deeply religious people.

The Fertile Crescent was the home of the ancient Sumerians—the builders of the first civilization in Mesopotamia. Their culture eventually outlasted them and became the basis for all later Babylonian civilization. The Sumerian way of life, style of writing, and religious customs were preserved in the Tigris-Euphrates river valley throughout ancient times by the kingdoms that followed—the Akkadian, Babylonian, and Assyrian empires.

The gods and goddesses of the Sumerians were adopted by successive Babylonian civilizations and although the names of these deities were often altered, their basic characteristics, personalities, symbolism, and cosmology changed little.

The Babylonians were an agricultural people who worshipped the natural forces of the universe that ruled the skies and governed the fertility of the earth. The relationship between gods and humans was compared to that between parents and children. There were cosmic gods, underworld gods, city gods, and gods of nature. There were also personal gods who were thought to favor specific individuals. Oftentimes the functions of these different classes of divinities overlapped. Certain gods were thought to be in charge of both cosmic forces and their earthly counterparts—the cities of Mesopotamia—whose existence was maintained by the surrounding farmland.

It was considered the duty of humanity to carry out the gods' will on earth, implementing a divine order that would secure the prosperity of the land and its people. The gods were honored with great temples that were the cultural and economic centers of the city-states. A city itself was considered the property of its primary deity, and the temple was the deity's earthly abode. It was in service to the gods that the Babylonians conceived many of their most important contributions to civilization, including writing, which developed from the need to keep track of temple assets. Every human endeavor, whether for peace, war, agriculture, or commerce, was performed for the benefit of the gods, whom the Babylonians depended upon for every aspect of their lives.

Below the realm of the celestial gods was the realm of spirits, both good and evil. Magical incantation developed as a method of appeasing friendly spirits and driving off malicious ones. As a result the practice of magic played a very important role in the religious expression of Mesopotamians. The average Babylonian employed the services of astrologers and magi (hereditary priest-magicians) for divination, healing, blessing of amulets and talismans, purification, cursing, warding off evil, etc. Private homes usually contained shrines to the owner's personal god or goddess, where prayers and sacrifices were made to attract the deity's favor.

It is these most ancient deities and spirits of "the Land between the Rivers" that are the subject of *Babylonian Tarot*.

The deck is comprised of eighty-three cards divided into two sections, the Major Arcana and the Minor Arcana. The Major Arcana consists of twenty-three Trump cards. The Minor Arcana contains sixty cards which are divided into two groups—the *pips*, which are the small or numbered cards, and the court cards.

Seventy-eight of the cards represent the traditional cards of the tarot with zodiacal, planetary, qabalistic, and elemental attributions that correspond with those of modern Hermetic decks such as the *Golden Dawn Magical Tarot*. There are five additional cards in this deck, including one extra trump (the card of Genesis) and four extra court cards. As in most other decks, the four court cards of the King, Queen, Prince, and Princess correspond to the four elements of Fire, Water, Air, and Earth. *Babylonian Tarot* includes a fifth court card, the *Kerub*, which represents the element of Spirit.

There are four suits: Wands, Cups, Arrows (comparable to Swords), and Disks (comparable to Pentacles). In general, Wands indicate Fire, great energy and dynamic power; Cups denote Water, creativity, fecundity, and pleasure; Arrows indicate Air, intellect, communication, mental faculties, and sometimes trouble; and Disks suggest Earth, material or worldly affairs, business, or money. A complete listing of attributions for every card is given in the appendix.

The Babylonians provided us with humanity's earliest written records of social, intellectual, and religious expression. Theirs was a long and rich history of human innovation and advancement, progress and set-backs, hopes and fears, successes and dreams. It is this rich source of knowledge that inspired the creation of *Babylonian Tarot,* correlating many of the major deities and legends of Mesopotamia to the wisdom of the tarot. Although perhaps not as well-known as emissaries from other pantheons, these heroic gods and goddesses are nonetheless every bit as fascinating as their later counterparts in Egypt, Greece, and Rome. The Fertile Crescent stills yields a rewarding harvest for those who wish to cultivate its productive soil.

Sandra Tabatha Cicero
Metatron House
First Day of Nisan (Vernal Equinox, 2004)

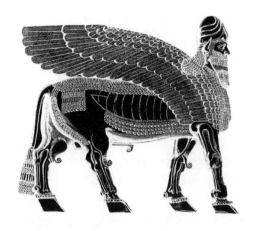

— The Trumps —

Genesis

This trump card has no number or attribution. This is because the card is meant to portray a time and space beyond words and numbers, before the concept of "zero" was even contemplated. It is meant to represent the birth of the universe—before the gods even existed—an event lost in the primordial mists prior to the concept of time. According to Babylonian legend, the *Apsu*, or primeval, sweet, freshwater sea symbolized by an abstract concept of a male deity, existed before anything else. Next was Tiamat, the chaos dragon or salt water sea. Within the Apsu, the heaven and the earth were formed. This card reflects the beginning of all beginnings, a portion of Babylonian cosmology that has been memorialized in the Hebrew Book of Genesis:

> *"In the beginning God created the heaven and earth. And the earth was without form, and void; and darkness was upon the face of the deep. And the Spirit of God moved upon the face of the waters."*[1]

The Babylonian Epic of Creation known as *Enuma Elish* ("When on High") describes the event this way:

> *When in the height heaven was not named,*
> *And the earth beneath did not yet bear a name,*
> *And the primeval Apsu, who begat them,*
> *And chaos, Tiamat, the mother of them both,*
> *Their waters were mingled together,*
> *And no field was formed, no marsh was to be seen;*
> *When of the gods none had been called into being,*

And none bore a name, and no destinies were ordained
Then were created the gods in the midst of heaven.[2]

The card shows the birth of the universe and the generation of the primeval gods. The head of an ancient deity appears against the backdrop of a storm-filled sky. The sea beneath has been whipped into a fury. A fetus appears in the middle of turbulent waves as the first of the gods are born.

Meaning: The absolute beginning or starting point. A new beginning. Commencement of a completely new outlook or phase of life. *(Reversed)*[3] Having to start completely over again. Fear of starting over. Entrenched in old ways of thinking.

0. The Fool: Enkidu

Enkidu was a wild-man created as a champion by the goddess Aruru to defeat Gilgamesh, who began his early career as a cruel dictator to the oppressed people of Uruk. As in the biblical account of the creation of the first man, Aruru creates Enkidu out of a lump of clay. According to some sources, Enkidu is occasionally depicted as a sort of satyr, with the head, arms, and body of a man, and the horns, ears, and legs of a beast—a type of bull-man known in Akkadian as *kusarikku* and in Sumerian as *gud-alim*, although in more recent times this image of Enkidu has been called into question by modern authors. Enkidu, whose body was covered with shaggy hair, knew nothing about the ways of man and civilization—he ate grass and ran with the wild creatures of the wilderness:

> . . . *with the gazelles he ate food in the night,*
> *with the beasts of the field he consorted in the day,*
> *with the creeping things of the waters his heart delighted. [. . .]*
> *with the beasts he drank of drink.*[4]

According to the *Epic of Gilgamesh*, Enkidu was discovered in the mountains by a hunter named Tsaidu who is exasperated to find that the wild man has destroyed his traps. The hunter informs Gilgamesh about the strength and swiftness of the wild man. By now Gilgamesh suspects the purpose for which Enkidu was created. He bids Tsaidu to return to Enkidu with a woman named Shamhat, a priestess of Ishtar. Shamhat uses her beauty and her charms to beguile and "tame" the wild man. For six days and seven nights Enkidu is only aware of his love for her. At the end of this time Enkudu finds that he has become a man, and he is no longer accepted by the gazelles and other animals as one of their own. He has become fully human. Shamhat takes him to the city of Uruk to learn the ways of civilization. When Enkidu arrives in Uruk, he fights and then befriends Gilgamesh.

The card of the Fool is attributed to Air. Here we see Enkidu, the satyr-like wild man as a primitive human, an innocent beast-like creature who is not yet a fully sentient being. He is at the crossroads between his animal nature represented by the green forest and leaping gazelle, and his full human potential symbolized by the golden city. The priestess Shamhat beckons Enkidu to leave the forest for the knowledge of civilization.

Meaning: Possibility. Idea, thought, potential, freedom, innocence, transition, the beginning, a new venture. Spirituality. The first breath. The first thought of manifestation. Choices yet to be made. (*Reversed*) Carelessness, folly, thoughtlessness, recklessness, instability, especially in material matters. The wrong choice is made.

1. The Magician: Ea

Ea (Sumerian *Enki*) was "Lord of Earth," king of the underworld, and ruler of the waters. He was the son of the sky god Anu and the primeval sea goddess Nammu. His primary domain was the Apsu, the freshwater abyss that was thought to surround the earth and provide water to all the springs and rivers. Ea was the main divinity of all fluid and watery substances—he was the god of the watery deep. The waters of the earth were a source of great abundance, fertility, and treasure, as well as knowledge. Therefore Ea became known as a god of wisdom and a good friend to humanity—creating man from clay and counseling and shielding human beings when other deities sought to harm them. It was Ea who helped humanity escape the destruction of the Great Flood in the story of *Atrahasis*.

Ea is the source and giver of wisdom. He taught humanity the crafts of building, farming, writing, and magic. As a god of medicine and the giver of the gifts of harvest and water, Ea's character was beneficent, humane, and protective. Ea's special function was to protect the human race against the harmful intentions of gods or spirits.

> *"There is no god conceived in so universal a manner as Ea. [. . .] His worship is not limited to any particular spot. All of Babylonia lays claim to him."*[5]

One of Ea's titles was *Nudimmud* or "he who creates." Another epithet was *nissiku* or "far-sighted." His other titles include "lord of wisdom," "maker of fate," "sage of the gods," and "lord of incantation." In the Sumerian story of

Enki and the World Order, the god of wisdom organizes every aspect of the civilized world by delegating the responsibilities for irrigation, fishing, agriculture, weaving, and other occupations to various lesser deities.

Ea is a compassionate and helpful god—he risks his life in the Underworld to rescue his twin sister Ereshkigal, he creates two genderless creatures to rescue Ishtar from the Land of the Dead, and he tells the god Ninurta how to kill the deceitful Anzu bird.

Ea guarded the sacred *me* (pronounced "may"), which were the divine decrees, ordinances, wisdom, and invocations that created civilization. The job of safeguarding the *me* was given to Ea by his older brother Ellil. Ea in turn distributed the *me* in an orderly fashion to humanity.

The god of wisdom is also said to have blessed the beautiful land of *Dilmun* (a form of Eden) with water and palm trees. Ea was especially associated with magic and incantations as indicated by the following excerpt from a Sumerian hymn of praise to Enki (Ea):

> *"Master of the commanding eye,*
> *the one who is seated on the earth,*
> *whose heart, far-reaching, knows all things,*
> *Enki, who spreads wisdom wide,*
> *Noble leader of the Anunna,[6]*
> *Expert who instituted incantations, word-rich,*
> *The one who keeps his eye on decisions,*
> *Guide who gives advice from sunrise to sunset,*
> *Enki, master of all the right commands:*
> *I want to praise you the way you should be praised."[7]*

Ea is third in line in the divine hierarchy, after his father Anu and his brother Ellil. Ea's wife was Aruru, and his children include Marduk, Tammuz, Damu, Nanshe, and Ningal.

The god Ea is sometimes portrayed as a goat with a fish's tail, or sometimes as a man with waves of water springing from his shoulders or from a vase which he holds. Animals that are sacred to him include the turtle and the antelope or deer, from which he receives the title "Stag of the Apsu."

The card of The Magician is attributed to Mercury. It shows Ea enthroned within the subterranean freshwater ocean of the Apsu. Streams of water with swimming fish flow from his shoulders. He holds a ram-headed staff, which is a symbol of his power.

Meaning: The act of experience. Invocation. Director of energy. Organization of thought. Thought becoming manifest. Strength of Will. The power of manifestation. Mastery, skill, wisdom, intelligence, adaptation, dexterity, self-determination, autonomy, the ability to control one's environment. Diplomacy. (*Reversed*) Trickery, lack of scruples, abuse of power. Controlled by outside forces. A liar or charlatan. Mental imbalance. Weak-willed. Indecisive and timid.

2. The High Priestess: Ishtar

Ishtar (Sumerian *Inanna*) was the most important goddess in the Babylonian pantheon. One of her titles was Belit[8] or "lady," the feminine form of Bel "lord." To all that she ruled, Ishtar had a positive and a negative side—kind one moment, harsh the next—not unlike the light and dark sides of the moon to which his card is attributed. A complex goddess of many roles, Ishtar, whose Sumerian name of Inanna meant "lady of heaven," had three distinct functions: (1) goddess of Venus, the morning and evening star, (2) goddess of love, and (3) goddess of war. It is possible that different aspects of Venus, as the morning and evening star, corresponded to the summer and winter seasons, and could have indicated the dual nature of the goddess.

Ishtar had many lovers and was not usually considered a mother goddess, having only one possible daughter, the goddess Sara. She had the power to arouse sexual desire and the ability to facilitate procreation in all creatures—she symbolized the fertility of the earth. Ishtar was "courtesan to the gods," and sacred prostitution formed an important part of her cult.

Although she often displayed her great kindness, she was also regularly cruel to her many lovers, and her affections were sometimes fatal. Her conflicted love for the harvest god Tammuz (Dumuzi) eventually caused his death. In the story of *The Descent of Ishtar to the Underworld,* the goddess enters the underworld because she wishes to obtain the knowledge of the place. In another version of the story, Ishtar decided to visit the underworld to witness the funeral rites of

Gugalanna, the Bull of Heaven, only to become her sister Ereshkigal's prisoner. Eventually she was freed and resurrected from death with a powerful magic spell by the god Ea.

In the tradition where Ishtar is seen as the daughter of the Moon god Sin, she was perceived as the goddess of war, who is fond of battle. She was said to stand beside favored monarchs as they fought.

The primary tradition concerning Ishtar in her city of Uruk made her the daughter of the god Anu. Here she was the starry goddess of love, predominantly a goddess of brilliance, light, and wisdom. It was she who tricked Ea and stole the holy *me* for her followers. In prayers she was often appealed to as a compassionate goddess who releases her followers from the afflictions of evil and disease. Ishtar became the focus of some of the highest and most sublime prayers written by the Babylonians. To them, she was *the* goddess.

This multi-faceted goddess ruled sexual love, fertility, revenge, warfare, resurrection, and initiation. She is usually represented as a winged goddess who wears a triple-horned crown and flowing robes, surrounded by stars. Her symbols are the lion, the rosette, and the eight-pointed star, which was an emblem of her celestial aspect as a sky-deity. Her other prominent symbol is the ring-post—a doorpost of a reed hut, usually with streamers, made of bundled reeds with the top end bent over to make a loop for the cross pole. The ring-post was an early symbol for the Ishtar's Sumerian name of Inanna, and was usually associated with her.

An Akkadian hymn praises the glory of the goddess:

Sing of the goddess, most awe-inspiring goddess,
Let her be praised, mistress of people,

Greatest of the Igigi-gods.[9] [. . .]
Her attributes are mighty, splendid, superb. [. . .]
Ishtar stands foremost among the gods,
Her word is the weightiest and prevails over theirs.
She is their queen, they relay her commands,
All of them bow down before her [. . .]
In their assembly her utterance is noble, surpassing,
She is seated among them as an equal to Anu their king,
She is wise in understanding and perception.
Together they make their decisions, she and her lord.[10]

The card of the High Priestess is attributed to the Moon. Here the goddess Ishtar is shown standing on a lion, her sacred animal, between two ring-posts that signify a doorway to the starry night sky. She holds the divine chaplet or string of beads.

Meaning: Consciousness. Awareness. Wisdom, knowledge, understanding, change, alternation, increase and decrease, fluctuation. Learning and teaching. Accurate intuition. Mystery. Hidden influences at work which bring hope. Secrets will be revealed at the proper time. (*Reversed*) Superficial knowledge, lack of foresight, ignorance, fuzzy thinking, prejudice, inability to make decisions.

3: The Empress: Aruru

Aruru (Sumerian Ninhursaga) was the goddess of the earth whose original name was thought to be *Ki* which meant "earth." She has numerous other names and titles, which may have originated as separate mother goddesses that later merged into one entity. These names and epitaphs include *Ninhursaga* "queen of the mountains," *Ninmah* "exalted lady," *Ninsikila*, and *Damkina* (Damgalnuna in Sumerian), *Mami* or *Mama* (clearly "mother"), *Nin-ziznak* "lady of the embryo," *Nin-bahar* "lady-potter," and *Nintur* "the lady who gives birth." As the wife of Anu, Aruru is the parent of many of the gods and goddesses, the great creative principle, and the archetypal Mother Goddess. Many Sumerian kings liked to refer to her as their mother, and claimed that they were nourished by her milk. She was called *Ninmena* or "lady of the diadem," because in Babylonian investiture rituals, she was said to place the crown on the head of the king.

Aruru was also known as the consort of Ea. She assisted Ea in the creation of humankind from clay and created eight new trees in the land of Dilmun, a pure and holy place which had previously been devoid of humans, animals, plants, or even water. It is for this reason that she is sometimes called *Nin-Dilmun*, or "lady of Dilmun." Ea blessed the paradisiacal land of Dilmun, to have plentiful water and palm trees.

According to the story of Dilmun, Ea and Aruru give birth to the goddess *Ninsar* or "lady plant." Through Ninsar, Ea sires Ninkur. Through Ninkur, Ea finally sires Uttu, the goddess of vegetation, upon Ninkur. Uttu bore eight new types of trees from Ea. The god of wisdom then consumed these tree-offspring and for this act he was cursed by Aruru, receiving one wound for each tree-child eaten. Eventually Aruru relents—she mates with Ea again and bears eight new tree-offspring, one to heal each of the deadly wounds.

In the *Epic of Gilagmesh*, the people of Uruk are abused by their king, the warrior Gilgamesh. They pray to the goddess Aruru for justice. The goddess agrees to create a champion for the oppressed people to fight against Gilgamesh. To do this the goddess forms a man (in the image of the god Anu) in her mind. Then she washes her hands and breaks off a piece of clay and with it she fashions Enkidu, the primitive man.

The following prayer invokes the beloved goddess and entreats her to eliminate a terrible disease from her devoted worshiper:

> *"O Damkina, mighty queen of all the gods,*
> *O wife of Ia (Ea), valiant thou art!*
> *O Ir-ni-na, mighty queen of all the gods,*
> *O wife of Ia, valiant thou art!*
> *Thou art great among the gods,*
> *Mighty is thy command! [. . .]*
> *. . . thou that dwellest in the Abyss,*
> *Oh lady of heaven and earth."*[11]

The goddess is often represented wearing a leafy crown or horned headdress, and holding a branch symbolizing fertility and regeneration. She is sometimes portrayed as a mid-wife or as a bare-breasted woman in a tiered skirt, carrying a child.

According to one legend, the name of the goddess was changed from *Ninmah* to *Ninhursaga* by her son Ninurta, to celebrate the creation of the mountains.

The card of The Empress is attributed to Venus. Here the goddess Aruru is shown bare-breasted and wearing a green tiered skirt and a leafy horned crown. To indicate her title as the Queen of the Mountains, a mountain peak is behind her, as well as the eight healing trees from the land of Dilmun. She holds a human figure that she is creating out of clay—the hero Enkidu.

Meaning: Feminine power. Power of manifestation. Beauty, happiness, pleasure, fruitfulness, fertility, abundance, harmony, marriage, motherhood. Comforts and luxuries. Love of nature. Sound understanding. *(Reversed)* Domestic upheaval. Sterility. Unplanned pregnancy. Over-indulgence. Loss of power, doubts and difficulties. Wasting of resources.

4. The Emperor: Marduk

Marduk was the firstborn son of Ea and patron god of the city of Babylon. The name of *Marduk* is said to mean "bull-calf of the sun," or "bull-calf of the storm," which points to his attribution as a god of thunder and tempest. Marduk became the central deity of the Babylonian pantheon and king of the gods. It was Marduk who organized the universe, fixed the course of the stars, and gave the gods their heavenly abodes. In the Babylonian creation story of *Enuma Elish*, Marduk served as the champion of the gods in a great cosmic battle between order and chaos, between the younger gods of light and the older gods of darkness. The epic *Enuma Elish* describes how the assembly of gods elevated Marduk to be their ruler and defend them against the chaos dragon Tiamat. Unanimously they proclaimed:

> *You are the most honored of the great gods,*
> *Your decree is unrivaled, your command is Anu.*
> *You, Marduk, are the most honored of the great gods,*
> *Your decree is unrivaled, your word is Anu.*
> *From this day your pronouncement shall be unchangeable.*
> *To raise or bring low—these shall be in your hand.*
> *Your utterance shall be true, your command shall be*
>   *unimpeachable.*
> *No one among the gods shall transgress your bounds! [. . .]*
> *O Marduk, you are indeed our avenger.*
> *We have granted you kingship over the universe entire.*
> *When you sit in Assembly your word shall be supreme.*[12]

In the later part of the second millennium, Marduk absorbed the attributes of most of the other Babylonian deities, including the storm god Ellil—taking over their various functions, characteristics, and even their names. In Tablet VI of the *Enuma Elish*, the gods declare the "Fifty Names of Marduk" some of which are: *Asarluhi,* god of incantation and light of the gods—the first name his father, Anu, gave him; *Marukka,* creator of the gods; *Marutukku,* supporter of the land; *Mershakushu,* the fierce yet merciful; *Asare,* creator of grain; *Shazu:* who knows the hearts of the gods, etc. The "Fifty Names of Marduk" were for the most part the names of gods he had usurped and which became different powers and aspects of his personality. This intentional absorption of numerous Babylonian gods into the many facets of Marduk shows a movement toward monotheism, although it never resulted in a denial of the existence of other gods and goddesses. Rather than replacing the other gods, Marduk became their supreme leader. Even Ea, the god of wisdom, integrated Marduk to himself:

> *(Ea heard and) . . . his spirit was rejoiced, (and he said):*
> *He whose name his fathers have made glorious,*
> *Shall be even as I, his name shall be Ea!*
> *The binding of all my decrees shall he control,*
> *All my commands shall he make known!*
> *By the name of 'Fifty' did the great gods*
> *Proclaim his fifty names, they made his path pre-eminent.*[13]

At the end of the *Enuma Elish*, Marduk's assimilation of the greatest of the gods is complete with the proclamation that Marduk is "the Enlil of the Gods."

In *The Religion of Babylonia and Assyria*, author Theophilus Pinches cites an ancient document wherein various Babylonian deities are identified with Marduk, in such a way as to make them simply forms in which the god revealed himself to humanity:

> . . . *Nergal is Merodach of war.*
> *Zagaga is Merodach of battle.*
> *Bêl is Merodach of lordship and domination.*
> *Nebo is Merodach of trading.*
> *Sin is Merodach the illuminator of the night.*
> *Samas? is Merodach of righteous things. . . .*[14]

Even more explicit references to Marduk's assimilation of other gods are asserted in ancient texts:

> *Marduk is Ninurta, the god of agriculture;*
> *He is Nergal, the god of battles;*
> *Zababa, the god of war;*
> *Nabu, the god of accountants;*
> *Enlil, the god of governing;*
> *Sin, the god who lights the night;*
> *Samas, the god of justice;*
> *And Adad, the god of rain.*[15]

The main celebration of Marduk's power was the *Akitu* or New Year's Festival which took place during the first twelve days of the month of Nisan (starting on March 20 or 21) at the time of the spring equinox. The festival included prayers and offerings to Marduk's statue, a priestly recital of the entire *Enuma Elish,* ritual cleansing of the temple, the divestiture and humbling of the King of Babylon before the statue of the great god, the procession or "visitation" of Marduk's statue to the sanctuary of the god Nabu, and a great banquet held in Marduk's honor.

Known as the "lord of life," Marduk was a gifted healer and a great magician who created man from the blood of the slain god Qingu. He was also considered a god of justice and compassion who cared about human beings—he was often invoked by his followers to banish evil and inequity. The visible manifestation of Marduk was *Nibiru,* the planet Jupiter, and he was called "Zeus" by ancient writers such as Herodotus. After he had risen to the top of the pantheon, Marduk was often simply called *Bel* or "Lord." Marduk was often invoked as a defender of good against evil by those who desired his protection.

Marduk is pictured as a mature, proud man usually striding off to do battle. He is often shown armed with a scimitar, thunderbolt, club, arrows, or other weapons. The god is sometimes said to have four ears and four eyes. His symbol is the *marru* or triangle-headed hoe, possibly alluding to his early origin as a god of agriculture. When he speaks, fire blazes from his mouth. His wife is the goddess Sarpanitu and his token animal is the snake-dragon.

The card of the Emperor is attributed to Aries. Here Marduk is shown armed to the teeth. In one hand he carries a bolt of lightning and in the other his symbol of the *marru.*

Meaning: Initiation of energy. Creative force. Worldly power. Leadership. Authority. Victory in war, conquest, ambition, accomplishment, goals met, protection, realization, development. Wise government. Stewardship. (*Reversed*) War, strife, problems with enemies, power dissipated, goals unreachable. Loss of power or position. Weakness.

5. The Hierophant: Nabu

Nabu (Biblical *Nebo*) was the Babylonian scribe god and the patron of writing, a role he took over from the Sumerian goddess Nisaba. Since much knowledge was passed on through writing, Nebu joined Ea and Marduk as a god of wisdom and intelligence, although few myths were written about him. His name is said to come from a root word meaning "to call," "proclaimer," or "herald" and he probably originated as a god of water. Nabu was sometimes identified with the planet Mercury. Known as the loyal son of Marduk and Sarpanitu and the grandson of Ea, Nabu was the patron god of Babylon's neighboring city of Borsippa. The worship of Nabu was wide-spread and long-lived—he was honored alongside his father Marduk at the New Year *Akitu* Festival. It is possible that in the final stages of Babylonian civilization, Nabu was beginning to supersede Marduk, just as Marduk had eclipsed the storm god Ellil. The Assyrians elevated the worship of the gentle Nabu over that of Marduk (so as not to anger their primary god Ashur, who would have considered the warrior Marduk a rival). Nabu's consort was Tashmetum, the goddess of hearing, who listened to prayers.

Nabu was said to engrave the future of every human being on the Tablet of Destiny, according to the decree of the gods. As the pronouncer of fate, Nabu has power over human existence. He is the all-knowing god who embodies the wisdom of the gods. He was also known as "lord of divination" and a patron of learning, science, and all knowledge. Other epitaphs include "lord of wisdom," "lover of justice," "light of the gods," "holder of the reed stylus," "holder of the scepter," "upholder of the world," and "chief priest of rites." His temple is called "the house of the scepter of the world." Nabu was considered the divine priest of the gods, as well as a benevolent deity and friend to human beings. Nebo bestowed the gift of writing to mankind. Tablet texts from King Ashurbanipal's library at Nineveh contain prayers to Nabu, asking the god to protect the text and curse anyone who steals it. Ashurbanipal, a lover of literature, invoked Nabu on thousands of the tablets of his library as "the opener of ears to understanding."

The name of Nabu was often used as a prefix to the names of kings such as *Nebu*chadnezzar. Devotion to this wise god impelled one Assyrian governor to engrave statues with the words "Trust in Nabu, do not trust in any other god." The popularity of Nabu is well documented in letters and prayers:

O hero, prince, first-born of Marduk!
O prudent ruler, offspring of Zarpanitu!
O Nabu, Bearer of the Tablet of the destiny of the gods, [. . .]
Darling of Ia (Ea), Giver of life!
Prince of Babylon, Protector of the living!
God of the hill of dwelling, the fortress of the nations,
the Lord of temples!
O son of the mighty prince Marduk, in thy mouth is justice![16]

Nabu's symbols were the clay tablet used by scribes to write on, the stylus and the wedge or writing chisel, all used for creating characters and words in cuneiform. The single wedge-shaped cuneiform mark was also his symbol. In Hellenistic times, Nabu was associated with Apollo, the god of prophesy.

The card of The Hierophant is attributed to Taurus. In this card all of the ancient cuneiform writing tools are seen behind the head of Nabu. The god is also shown with his token animal, the snake-dragon or *mushussu*, a creature also sacred to his father, Marduk. Nabu wears the horned head-dress of divinity and holds his hands in an ancient gesture of priesthood.

Meaning: Inner illumination. Channel for spiritual wisdom and instruction. The great teacher. Mercy, goodness, kindness, inspiration, manifestation, explanation, the quest for truth, moral courage, spiritual inclination. Religious. (*Reversed*) Extreme conservative, bound to orthodoxy. Has a need to conform or please. Weakness, loss of moral authority, overly kind. "Too much Mercy is but Weakness and fading out of the Will."

6. The Lovers: Ishtar and Tammuz

Mesopotamian religion viewed the sexual union between male and female as essential to the productivity of the land. Sex was also considered pleasing to the gods, particularly to the goddess Ishtar, the goddess of love and erotica. The Babylonians explained the creation of the universe as the result of a series of divine marriages between pairs of deities. This idea was the beginning of the tradition known as the *hieros gamos* or sacred marriage. The divine couple associated with this sacred marriage was Ishtar and Tammuz.

Tammuz (Sumerian *Dumuzi* or "good son"), son of Ea and the cow goddess Ninsun, was the royal shepherd of Uruk. He probably originated as a king who became deified. Tammuz is associated not only with herdsmen and their flocks but also with vegetation, particularly the date palm. An Akkadian hymn describes Tammuz as "Shepherd and lord, husband of Ishtar the lady of heaven, lord of the under-world, lord of the shepherd's seat."[17] He is often referred to as the "bridegroom." Like Gilgamesh, Tammuz is a mortal demi-god.

Tammuz falls in love with the goddess and attempts to court her. In one tradition, Inanna-Ishtar favors the farmer god Enkimdu over Tammuz before changing her mind. In another tradition, Tammuz is immediately accepted as Ishtar's husband. A series of joyous love songs celebrated the union of the divine couple:

> *Inanna, at her mother's command,*
> *Bathed herself, anointed herself with goodly oil,*

Covered her body with the noble pala-garment,
Took along the [. . .], her dowry,
Arranged the lapis lazuli about her neck,
Grasped the seal in her hand.
The Lordly Queen waited expectantly,
Dumuzi pressed open the door,
Came forth into the house like the moonlight,
Gazed at her joyously,
Embraced her, kissed her.[18]

The love affair between Ishtar and Tammuz, like many human relationships, was complex and volatile. In the story of *Ishtar's Descent into the Underworld*, the goddess is forced to choose someone to take her place in the Underworld. Angered that Tammuz seemed unmoved by her plight, she chooses him. As a result Tammuz had to spend six months of the year in the Land of the Dead, resulting in the change of season. Tammuz's death signaled the end of the harvest and the arrival of the harsh Babylonian summer when crops and milk-herds dry up. The growing season began again when Tammuz was released and his sister Gestinana consigned to a six-month stay in the Underworld.

The fertility of humans, animals, and crops was thought to depend on the sexual union of Ishtar and Tammuz. Thus, the annual celebration of the hieros gamos included a ritual marriage between the human king and a priestess as living representatives of the shepherd king and the goddess of love. The priestess representing Ishtar took a ritual bath and adorned herself in her finest regalia to receive the king. She sang passionate love songs to her royal lover (in the following case, the bridegroom was a monarch named Shu-Sin):

Bridegroom, dear to my heart,
Goodly is your pleasure, honey-sweet;
Lion, dear to my heart,
Goodly is your pleasure, honey-sweet;
You have captivated me, I stand trembling before you.
Bridegroom, I would be carried off by you to the bedchamber;
*   [. . .]*
Your spirit—I know where to cheer your spirit,
Bridegroom, sleep in our house till dawn,
Your heart—I know where to gladden your heart.
Lion, sleep in our house till dawn,
You, because you love me,
Lion, give me pray of your caresses,
The lord my god, the lord my good genie,
My Shu-Sin who gladdens the heart of Enlil,
Give me pray of your caresses.[19]

The ritual marriage between these two surrogates was thought to mystically accomplish the union of Ishtar and Tammuz. After the sacred marriage was consummated, Ishtar "fixed the destiny" of the king for the ensuing year, granting him the divine power necessary to ensure the productivity of the land. A great banquet and celebration followed.

The card of The Lovers is attributed to Gemini. In this card Ishtar is shown welcoming the advances of Tammuz, who approaches the goddess bearing a golden chalice. The rainbow and the peahen are meant to be symbols of wholeness and harmony.

Meaning: Love, attraction, union, cooperation, harmony. Integration of the Higher and the lower. Union of spiritual and material. Divine love. Freedom through unity. Fusion. Bonding. Inspiration. Intuition. Insight. Motivation. Choice and responsibility. Wise choice. (*Reversed*) Conflict and division. Interference from others. Break-up. Infidelity. Wrong choice or inability to choose.

7. The Chariot: Adad

Sometimes called *Hadad, Addu,* or *Adda,* (Sumerian *Iskur*), Adad eventually usurped Ellil's position as principle god of storm. He was primarily a weather god—the lord of the elements and shaker of the earth. The cuneiform sign for his Sumerian name of *Iskur* was the same as the sign for "wind" while his Akkadian name of *Adad* means "thunderer."

The son of either Anu or Ellil and twin brother of Ea, Adad had powers that were both destructive and beneficial. He was responsible for floods as well as destructive storms, floods, and hail, but he also had a positive side as a god of fertile rains and streams—especially in areas of Mesopotamia where rainfall was crucial to agriculture. As a divine overseer of celestial and terrestrial sources of water, Adad brought fertility to the land and blessings to the cities. He supplied the wells, fields, and irrigation canals with life-giving water. Because his powers could be either harmful or beneficial to humans, it was considered very important to win his favor.

Some of his other titles were "lord of the clouds," "lord of rain," and "lord of abundance, the controller of the floodgates of heaven and earth." When crops failed it was due to Adad's wrath. He could make thorns grow instead of grain. Adad's lion-like "roar" was terrifying for it usually signaled misfortune.

As a god of oracles, divination, and judgment, Adad was also known as the "lord of foresight" who could read the future. His companion was the goddess Sala.

In the West Semitic or Canaanite pantheon, Adad became assimilated with other gods such as the storm god *Ba'lu* or "lord" (the Biblical *Ba'al*) and the grain god *Dagon*, father of Ba'al.[20] In Assyria he became very popular—he gained the epitaph *Ramman*, "the thunderer" (the Biblical *Rimmon*) and became a god of war who was invoked to bring a raging tempest down on the head of the enemy. An Assyrian hymn to Ramman describes how the other gods would flee before the storm god's fury:

> *The mighty mountain, thou hast overwhelmed it.*
> *At his anger, at his strength,*
> *At his roaring, at his thundering,*
> *The gods of heaven ascend to the sky,*
> *The gods of the earth ascend to the earth,*
> *Into the horizon of heaven they enter,*
> *Into the zenith of heaven they make their way.*[21]

One of Adad's centers of worship was a Babylonian town called Karkara, which also used the same sign as the god's name. Another center of worship was the town of Yamhad (Aleppo) where the weapon which Adad used to smite the Sea (*Yam*) was said to be kept. Adad's battle with the primeval sea is yet another retelling of the Epic of Creation wherein Marduk fought the sea dragon Tiamat in a great cosmic battle between good and evil, order and chaos, light and dark. The cosmic conflict between Adad/Ba'al and the Sea underwent yet another change when the Biblical authors of the Old Testament borrowed the attributes, personality, and even the legendary exploits of Babylonian storm gods for their own warrior god, Yahweh.

Adad is usually depicted with a thunderbolt in each hand and standing upon a bull or a lion-dragon, both of which are his totem animals. He sometimes carries a mace, a double-ax, sheaves of grain, or holds the reigns of his mount. The god is often shown standing in his chariot, riding into battle.

The lion-dragon or lion-griffin, is a creature which has the head and forelimbs of a lion, and the hind-legs, tail, and wings of a bird. In recent years some sources have suggested that this type of creature may have been known as the *umu na'iru* or "roaring weather beast." Storm clouds were referred to as "Adad's bull-calves."

The card of The Chariot is attributed to Cancer. It depicts the storm god in his chariot, armed with a lightning bolt. His chariot is ornamented with the figure of the lion-dragon, one of his sacred animals. Storm clouds, symbolized by the heads of bulls, gather around him.

Meaning: Triumph, conquest, victory over enemies. Progress through one's own efforts. Mastery of opposing forces. Guided by Spirit. Movement and travel. (*Reversed*) Conflict, defeat. Overpowered by enemies. Revenge. Unethical victory. Ruthlessness.

8. Strength: Gilgamesh

The *Epic of Gilgamesh* is one of the oldest pieces of world literature. There are four cuneiform versions of the epic, with the most recent version written on twelve clay tablets in the first millennium B.C.E. The epic centers around *Gilgamesh*, a mighty Sumerian king of the city of Uruk—who may have been a living ruler who was deified after his death.

Gilgamesh was the son of the warrior-king Lugalbanda and the wise cow goddess Ninsun. He is said to have built the walls of the city Uruk, and the Eanna ("house of Anu") temple compound there, dedicated to the goddess Ishtar. As a demigod who is one-third human and two-thirds divine, Gilgamesh is an unrivaled warrior:

> *Supreme over other kings, lordly in appearance,*
> *he is the hero, born of Uruk, the goring wild bull.*
> *He walks out in front, the leader,*
> *and walks at the rear, trusted by his companions.*
> *Mighty net, protector of his people,*
> *raging flood-wave who destroys even walls of stone!*
> *Offspring of Lugalbanda, Gilgamesh is strong to*
> *perfection. . . .*[22]

In the beginning of the epic, Gilgamesh is a mighty ruler, but one who has a penchant for acting in an arrogant fashion—he harasses young men and sleeps with their brides before marriage. When the people of Uruk pray for help, the goddess Aruru creates a champion for them—Enkidu the wild man—to battle Gilgamesh. After fighting it out, however, Enkidu and Gilgamesh become friends. They go off on many adventures together, including the killing of the monster Humbaba, guardian of the Cedar Forest. They also battle and kill the rampaging Bull of Heaven who was sent to destroy the city of Uruk. However, the gods are unhappy with the killing of Humbaba and the Celestial Bull and decide that there is a price to be paid for such actions. They decree that Enkidu must die.

Enkidu dreams of his own death; as the dream predicted, he sickens and dies. Gilgamesh is devastated. He mourns the loss of his friend and becomes obsessed with the nature of life and death. He fears for his own mortality and embarks on a quest to learn the secret of eternal life. Eventually his wanderings lead him to find Utnapishtim, the survivor of the Great Flood, the only human who was ever granted immortality by the gods. Utnapishtim tells Gilgamesh where to find a plant that restores youth. Gilgamesh obtains the plant but then losses it—squandering his only chance to gain eternal youth. At the end of Gilgamesh's journey, he returns to his city of Uruk. For the first time, he really appreciates the city and its people. He accepts his own human mortality, and is finally at peace with himself, becoming a responsible leader of his people—his legacy will live on through them and through the civilization he created. In his youth the arrogant Gilgamesh was a mighty warrior who fought and vanquished many creatures. But his *true strength* lay in his ability to grow and learn.

The last version of the *Epic of Gilgamesh* added a twelfth and final tablet to the previous eleven. In this tablet, the ghost of Enkidu visits Gilgamesh and describes the Underworld and its inhabitants in detail. This story clearly insinuates that

Gilgamesh will die, but he will soon become a god—a judge in the Underworld. In this way he will gain immortality, but only as a god, not as a human being.

The character of Gilgamesh occurs more often than any other figure in this deck. Here he is the archetypal hero who goes on a journey of transformation, endurance, and seeking after knowledge. He experiences both victory and sorrow, finds a friend and loses him, rebuffs one deity and prays out of fear to another, loses himself and finds himself, and evolves from a selfish thug to a noble and compassionate ruler. In his pursuit of an illusive immortality, he comes to appreciate what he already has, and in the end he becomes immortal by becoming an underworld god. Gilgamesh's quest to find immortality is analogous to the journey of all spiritual seekers who desire to find the true spark of immortality which exists within us all. Like Gilgamesh, we are changed for the better by the experiences of the journey within.

Gilgamesh is often shown in Babylonian art either carrying or wrestling a lion. He is also sometimes shown wrestling the Bull of Heaven. There is a solar connection to Gilgamesh as well, for the hero prays to the sun God Shamash, who acts as his patron and protector.

The card of Strength is attributed to Leo. It depicts the hero Gilgamesh fighting a lion. A ziggurat or stepped pyramid is seen in the background.

Meaning: Strength, fortitude, triumph, energy, action, determination, resolve. success. Force of Will. Harnessed force.

Passions under the control of the Will. Courage to take risks. Ability to endure hardship. Spiritual power overcoming material power. Reconciliation with a former enemy. (*Reversed*) Abuse of power, failure, weakness, discord.

9. The Hermit: Anu

Anu (Sumerian *An*), the god of heaven, was the main god of the pantheon until 2500 B.C.E. His name meant "sky" and "heaven," which were considered one and the same, and he resided in the uppermost region of the heavenly realm far away from the affairs of human beings. Anu was the father of two groups of gods, the *Igigi* (celestial gods) and the *Anunnaki* (chthonic gods). His titles include "father of the gods," "founder of kingship," and "lord of creation." Anu is the supreme Lord of the Firmament and the god who sustains the universe.

In the Babylonian epic *Enuma Elish*, the story of Creation unfolds as a series of births—the generations of gods. In the beginning, nothing existed but a watery chaos made up of the *Apsu*, the sweet waters, *Tiamat*, the dragon of the sea, and *Mummu*, the clouds and mist. From this combination of different waters came the birth of two primordial beings named *Lahmu* and *Lahamu*, deities of fertility and expanse. These two entities in turn sired the deities *Anshar* and *Kishar*, both aspects of the horizon. This pair gave birth to Anu, the great sky god, and other generations of deities followed.

The main principle of creation and founder of the cosmos, Anu was the father and supreme king of the older generation of gods. According to one tradition, Anu took precedence over heaven when it was divided from the earth by Anu's son Ellil, when the universe as we know it was established. Most of the other deities of the Sumerian pantheon honored Anu as their father or chief. His first consort was Antu ("female heaven"). Another companion was Ki or Aruru, the great Mother Earth goddess. Anu was the father of Ellil, Adad, Ishtar, and others. With the primeval water goddess Nammu, he fathered Ea.

Anu symbolized power, protection, justice, and judgment, and he was often represented by a horned tiara on a throne or altar. His royal emblems were the scepter, the horned cap, the crook or shepherd's staff, and the staff of command. His army, which was used to destroy the wicked, were the stars that he had created (called the "soldiers of Anu"). Never leaving the heavenly regions, Anu occasionally traversed a portion of the sky reserved only for him called "Anu's way," located in the uppermost part of the heavens. The "Way of Anu" was also the sun's ecliptic. More benevolent toward monarchs than to commoners, Anu bestowed kingship on individual rulers. He was the supreme divine authority among the gods—he presided over the fate of the universe and its inhabitants. Anything he put into words became reality. It was Anu who was first in charge of the holy *me* or divine ordinances before he turned them over to his son Ellil and eventually to Ea. A remote, aloof, and distant god, Anu sometimes intervenes to change destiny, but more often than not, he tends to stay out of both human and godly affairs. This is because the supreme "god of heaven" was to some extent an abstract concept.

In nearly all periods of Babylonian history, Anu was one of the most important cosmic gods of the Mesopotamian pantheon. However, the attributes of this shadowy deity were vague and obscure and he was rarely ever depicted in Babylonian art. Most often he was merely symbolized by the image of a multi-horned cap, the headdress of divinity, placed upon an altar.

The Greeks associated Anu with Zeus and Ouranos.

The card of the Hermit is attributed to Virgo. Here the Hermit is depicted as the misty form of the male deity, Anu. Before him is his symbol, the horned cap on an altar, while behind him is a crook.

Meaning: Inner wisdom. Introspection. Hidden Truth. Divine inspiration. Divine Intervention. Message from the Higher. Vibration. The Supreme Will. Help and inspiration from the Higher. A helpful guide or wise councilor. Prudence, moderation, withdrawal, solitude, introspection, caution, journeying, seeking. Discretion and silence. (*Reversed*) Misinformation, lies, concealment, fraud. Immaturity. Rejection of good advice. Refuses offers of assistance.

10. The Wheel: Tablet of Destiny

The Tablet of Destiny was a divine clay tablet of cuneiform writing impressed with seals, upon which the fates of all humans and gods were decreed. Whoever was in possession of the Tablet controlled the fate of the world—whatever they commanded was destined to happen. Owning the Tablet was considered the same as ruling the universe and having power over the affairs of humans and deities alike. The Tablet was thought of as a kind of authoritative contract or legally binding document. The god who owned the Tablet often wore it on his breast.

In the *Enuma Elish* the Tablet first appears in the possession of the chaos dragon Tiamat, although it is inferred that the Tablet was stolen from the sky god Anu. Planning for battle against the younger gods, Tiamat gives the Tablet to Qingu, the leader of her army. Marduk eventually slays Tiamat, takes the Tablet from Qingu, and returns it to Anu.

The wise god Nabu is said to engrave the future of every human being on the Tablet of Destiny.

In the *Epic of Anzu*, the Tablet of Destiny has been passed from Anu to Ellil. A monstrous lion-headed eagle named Anzu manages to deceive Ellil and steal the Tablet. The whole of existence is threatened by this act. The gods chose the warrior-farmer Ninurta to be their champion and go after the thief. After some difficulty caused by Anzu's possession of the Tablet, Ninurta kills Anzu and returns the Tablet to Ellil. With the Tablet back in the hands of its rightful owner, the fate of the universe is restored to balance.

The card of the Wheel is attributed to the planet Jupiter. It shows the Tablet of Destiny, covered in cuneiform writing. In front of the Tablet is a wheel that represents an Assyrian city—the outer circle is a stone wall with battlements. The city is divided into quarters by two streets. Inside the city, people are going about their daily business, preparing food.

At the top of the wheel is a Babylonian sphinx, a winged, human-headed lion figure that was often used to guard gateways. Here the sphinx is a guardian of the heavens and a representative of the Higher Genius.

Below the wheel is *Arali*, the Babylonian underworld. Three galla demons surround a man, ready to carry him off. Here the man is used to represent the Lower Self assailed by various impulses of the unconscious.

Meaning: Time. Destiny. The rotation and cycling of human incarnation. Perpetual motion. Karma—bringing past deeds into the present and on into the future. Good Fortune and happiness. Success. Promotion. Increase. Unexpected turn of luck. The beginning of a new cycle. Fluctuation. The Spiritual guiding the material. (*Reversed*) Failure. The material ruling the spiritual. A turn for the worst. Bad karma. Payback.

11. Justice: Nanshe

The Sumerian goddess *Nanshe* or *Nash* was the daughter of Enki (Ea). She was the sister of the warrior god Ningirsu and the goddess of writing Nisaba, who is usually at her side to record her judgments. Her center of worship was Sirara near Lagash in south east Sumer, where she played an important role in realm of humanity's moral and ethical conduct. Nanshe was considered a great administrator and overseer of social justice—caring for widows, orphans, and the poor. In one hymn dedicated to her, the goddess is described as judging humanity on New Year's Day, giving comfort to the weak and meting out punishment to the wicked.

> *Who knows the orphan, who knows the widow,*
> *Knows the oppression of man over man,*
> *is the orphan's mother,*
> *Nanshe, who cares for the widow,*
> *Who seeks out [. . .] justice [. . .] for the poorest [. . .]*
> *The queen brings the refugee to her lap,*
> *Finds shelter for the weak.*[23]

The hymn describes Nanshe's functions:

> *To comfort the orphan, to make disappear the widow,*
> *To set up a place of destruction for the mighty,*
> *To turn over the mighty to the weak . . .,*
> *Nanshe searches the heart of the people.*[24]

Another of her duties was to check the accuracy of weights and measures.

Nanshe was also associated with divination and the science of *oeniromancy* or the ability to interpret dreams as indicated by her titles of "Interpreter of Dreams" and "Diviner of the gods."

Symbols of the goddess Nanshe include birds, fishes, and water, and her name is written by a composite sign for "house" and "fish."

The card of Justice is attributed to Libra. Here the goddess Nanshe is seated on a throne. She has her left arm around an orphaned child, protecting and consoling him. In her right hand she holds the Rod and Ring, symbols that denote straightness and completeness—divine right and justice. Above her is the disk of the Sun god Shamash, the primary god associated with the idea of justice.

Meaning: Fairness, integrity, equity. Proper balance, and equilibrating action. Power and force. Necessary adjustment. Triumph of the righteous. Legal proceedings. Judgment, arbitration, negotiated agreement. Compensation. (*Reversed*) Abuse of power. Excessive severity. Imbalance. Inequity, bias, injustice. Legal problems.

12. The Hanged Man: Tammuz

Tammuz (Sumerian *Dumuzi,* "the good son") was briefly introduced in the card of The Lovers. Known as a god of herdsmen and flocks, Tammuz was also associated with crops, spring vegetation, date palms, and barley. Husband of the goddess Ishtar, Tammuz represents the spring growth of new life in all of nature. His other titles include "divine shepherd" and "bridegroom." Tammuz is the very first "dying-and-rising" god to be named in recorded history.

The death of Tammuz is tied to the story of Inanna-Ishtar's descent into the underworld. When Ishtar was released from the underworld, she was still held under a pledge to Ereshkigal (the goddess of death) to find someone who would take her place. Angry that Tammuz had not mourned her when she went missing, Ishtar chooses him to take her place in the land of the dead. Two *galla* demons who had accompanied the goddess seize Tammuz. In distress, the shepherd god raises his hands and cries out to Shamash, the solar god of justice. Shamash takes pity on Tammuz and causes him to escape the demons' grasp.

Weeping, Tammuz flees across the steppes. He falls asleep and dreams of his own death. He seeks refuge in the house of his sister Gestinana, goddess of the vine, who interprets his foreboding dream. As the galla demons close in, Tammuz hides in the tall grass. The demons go to Gestinana's house to find him. At first they try to bribe Gestinana into revealing where Tammuz is hiding. When that fails, they resort to torture, but Gestinana's silence is steadfast. The shepherd's hiding place is finally revealed by a treacherous friend. The galla capture Tammuz a second time, and he again cries out to Shamash for help. The sun god intervenes a second time on his behalf—he changes Tammuz into a gazelle which escapes from the demons' grasp.

Tammuz attempts to hide in his sister's sheep pen but he is caught a third time by the galla, who beat him. Naked and bound, Tammuz is dragged off to the underworld:

> *The galla seized Dumuzi.*
> *They surrounded him.*
> *They bound his hands.*
> *They bound his neck.*
> *The churn was silent.*
> *No milk was poured.*
> *The cup was shattered.*
> *Dumuzi was no more.*
> *The sheepfold was given to the winds.*[25]

After Tammuz is taken away, Ishtar's anger at him dissipates. She is filled with remorse at the lost of her husband. Gestinana, also stricken with grief, vows to share her brother's fate. Together, the two goddesses go to the Underworld and find Tammuz crying. The goddesses comfort him and Ishtar decrees that Tammuz will stay in the underworld for six months of the year, and Gestinana will take his place there for the remaining six months.

The Sumero-Babylonian story of Tammuz in the underworld is the first recorded instance of the agricultural sacrifice mythos, which has been repeated numerous times in other ancient cultures. Tammuz was the life-blood of the fields and of the sheepfold. His death coincided with the annual harvesting of crops and the beginning of the harsh, barren season that withered vegetation and dried up the milk of sheep and goats. The return of the annual growing season signaled Tammuz's release from the netherworld back into the land of the living. The plowing of fields, the blossoming of trees, and the production of fruit was a sign of Tammuz's vitality returning.

Ritualized lamentation for the death of the shepherd god was widespread in the ancient world. The Biblical Book of Ezekiel mentions that women wailed over the death of Tammuz at the northern gate of the temple in Jerusalem. The Greeks associated Tammuz with Adonis.

The card of the Hanged Man shows the god Tammuz between two galla demons who are about to take him into the underworld. This card is attributed to the element of water.

Meaning: Sacrifice, especially self-sacrifice. Self-denial. Suspended animation. Trance-state. A period of withdrawal. Introspection. Listening to the Inner Self. Pause. Delayed decision. Reversal. Wisdom and intuition. Sacrificing something in order to gain something better. (*Reversed*) False prophecy. A martyr complex. Petty sacrifices. Rejects the guidance of Spirit. Arrogance and ego-inflation. Psychic or mental disorder.

13. Death: Ereshkigal

Ereshkigal, whose name meant "Queen of the Great Below" was the goddess of the underworld. Her Akkadian name was *Allatu,* which is said to mean "strength." The daughter of Anu and Ki and twin sister of Ea, Ereshkigal was originally a sky or grain goddess who was kidnapped by the primeval dragon Kur. She later took the underworld for her abode. Ereshkigal's attendant deities are Namtar, a god of disease, and her scribe, Belit-seri.

The Mesopotamians had several names for the underworld including: *Arali, Irkalla, Kukku, Kurnugi, Ekur, Kigal, Ganzir, Kur,* and *Ersetu.* Titles for the netherworld included "the land of no return," "the ground," "the desert," "the earth," and "the lower world." The land of the dead was imagined to have a guarded front gate that opened up to a staircase leading into an underground chamber. Arali was thought to be situated on a level that was even lower than the Absu, the freshwater sea located below the earth.

The Babylonian underworld is usually described as a dark and desolate place where the spirits of the dead wander in a type of dreary half-life. Death was considered the great equalizer, for proud kings fared no better than slaves in Arali. The Underworld was also home to various chthonic deities and a few demons such as the galla whose job was to fetch the dead.

Ereshkigal is often referred to as the dark sister of Ishtar—she can be equated to the shadowy alter-ego. Her behavior was aggressive and ferocious—Ereshkigal's rage, once invoked, was boundless and primeval. The bold descent of Ishtar into the land of Arali so infuriated Ereshkigal that she struck her sister dead and hung her body on the wall for three days before Ishtar was rescued and brought back to life. Ereshkigal is a goddess of strong passions—the story of Nergal-Erra's courtship of the dark goddess is one of fiery romance.

The underworld is often used as a metaphor for the unconscious mind with all its primal fears, jealousies, unwanted desires, and repressed psychic impulses. It has been suggested that dark goddess Ereshkigal symbolizes all of the raw, instinctual impulses that have been shunned and shoved into the subconscious. This accounts for the rage of the goddess and the fear she inspires. If we try to ignore and suppress our own unwanted psychic material, it will only leak out in unhealthy and undesirable ways. Ereshkigal will not be ignored. She forces us to see the truth about ourselves, even though the truth may be unpleasant. Eventually we must confront the dark goddess in the underworld, just as Ishtar did. Only by shining the light of day into the dark crevasses of our own mental workings can we, like Ishtar, gain true knowledge of the underworld—and complete knowledge of our own inner selves.

The card of Death is attributed to Scorpio. This card portrays the goddess Ereshkigal seated on a throne in her underworld kingdom of the dead.

Meaning: Transformation. Transmutation. Metamorphosis. Alteration. Sudden or involuntary change. A situation that cannot be avoided. Destruction that is actually a blessing in disguise. Release of the outmoded. Birth or renewal. Change

of one form for another. Cycle of death and rebirth. Purification. (*Reversed*) Stagnation, inertia. Resistance to positive
change. Failure, destruction.

14. Temperance: Tree of Life

One of the most elegant motifs in Babylonian art is the stylized tree often called the Tree of Life. Its design displays perfect balance and symmetry. The Tree is located in the center of a garden paradise and is usually shown flanked by protective genies such as the eagle-headed spirit, or with the winged disk above its apex.

Some have suggested that the Tree of Life was originally a grapevine since the Sumerian term for grapevine was *geshtin*, which had the dual meanings of "tree" and "life." Others maintain that the Tree is a date palm covered with a grapevine trellis. In any event, it is a symbol of power—its fruit or sap provides life-giving benefits.

The Tree of Life is usually associated with the ritual of kingship, sometimes called the "cone-smearing" ceremony, during which the king was magically protected, purified, and anointed. In this manner, the king was identified with the Tree and its powers of fertility and fruitfulness—the king became the distributor of the Tree's benefits, including life itself, to the land and the nation.

Many authors have speculated that the Babylonian Tree of Life along with its protective Kerubim was the model for the two Trees in the Biblical story of Genesis: the Tree of Life and the Tree of the Knowledge of Good and Evil.

The card of Temperance is attributed to the sign of Sagittarius. It shows the Tree of Life in full blossom. Its roots are anchored in the earth and its blossoms extend upward, nearly reaching the winged disk of Shamash, the sun god, whose beneficent rays shine down on the Tree.

Meaning: Balance and equilibrium. Fusion. Combination. Balancing of volatile energies. Tempering of opposites. Uniting. Amalgamation. Material action. Good management, coordination. Harmonious partnership. Diplomacy. Necessary trial and temptation for the sake of balance and union. (*Reversed*) Bad combination or unfortunate alliance. Competing interests. Bungling and ineptitude. Imbalance, disharmony.

15. The Devil: Lamastu

One of the most feared entities in the Babylonian pantheon was *Lamastu* (Sumerian *Dimme*). More than just a "demoness" as some have called her, Lamastu was a type of demi-goddess and the daughter of Anu. Unlike demons, who were usually neutral and only committed harmful acts when commanded by the gods to do so, Lamastu enjoyed committing evil for the shear pleasure of it. Lamastu was particularly cruel towards young children—she was responsible for causing miscarriages and crib deaths among infants. She was also responsible for causing disease and nightmares. One of her epitaphs is "she who erases." Lamastu was the prototype for what would later become the earliest vampire and succubus legends. The Greeks associated her with Lamia.

A whole series of rituals were designed to protect pregnant women and nursing mothers against Lamastu. Babylonian women would hang protective plaques by their doorways to keep her out. In an effort to "fight fire with fire," women often wore amulets of another demon—Pazuzu, the evil wind demon who in this case had a beneficial side—he was the mortal enemy of Lamastu and had the power to chase her back to her underworld lair.

The card of The Devil is attributed to the sign of Capricorn. Here Lamastu is portrayed as having the head of a lioness, the ears and teeth of a donkey, the feet of an eagle, a hairy body with naked breasts, and bloodstained hands with long claws. A piglet and a dog suckle from her breasts and in her hands she holds deadly serpents. She stands upon her totem animal, a donkey, in a boat that sails along the river of the underworld.

Meaning: Natural generative force. Material Force. Possessions. Sensuality. Sexual force and reproduction. Hedonism. Material temptation or excess. Self-deception. Illusion. Distorted perceptions. Mirth. (*Reversed*) Lust for Power. Violence. Deceit. Appetites out of control. Self-destructive behaviors. Addiction. Obsession.

16. The Tower: Marduk and Tiamat

The theme of this card is a great battle in heaven between the powers of light and darkness. The Babylonian creation story *Enuma Elish* explains that a generational gap eventually formed between the older gods and the younger, active gods. A conflict occurred wherein the most ancient god Apsu regretted having sired such noisy children and vowed to obliterate them. When the wise Ea learned of this, he cast a magic spell over Apsu which caused him to fall asleep. Ea then killed the ancient one and established a portion of the world as it now is—the waters of Apsu sank down, and over them Ea established the earth. This was the first great victory of order over chaos.

In time the chaos dragon *Tiamat* convinced her allies to avenge the death of her husband Apsu, and negotiations between the two factions fell through. Because of the impending crisis, the gods decided to elect a champion to lead them in the fight against Tiamat and her army of monster serpents and fierce dragons. They chose Marduk, son of Ea, who armed himself with all the weapons of a storm god: thunder and lightning, bow and arrow, a mace, a net, four winds, seven storms, and an evil, disease-carrying wind.

At the sight of the great Marduk in his chariot, Tiamat's army fled—only Tiamat herself stood her ground. Marduk forced her to swallow the evil wind and then killed her with an arrow. He split her body into two halves, one of which he used to create the starry heavens, the other to create the earth. He posted guards over her and bade them "to allow not her waters to escape." Tiamat's saliva become the clouds and her two eyes became the rivers of the Tigris and the Euphrates. After banishing the waters of chaos and establishing order, Marduk was enthroned as the Sovereign of Babylon and of the universe with the proclamation *Marduk sarru*, "Marduk is King."

The card of The Tower is attributed to the planet Mars. It depicts the cosmic battle between Marduk and Tiamat raging in the night sky. Tiamat is usually portrayed as a the lion-dragon—the *umu na'iru* or "roaring weather beast." In this card, the war between order and chaos has filled the heavens, and Marduk's lightning bolt has struck a ziggurat or stepped pyramid, splitting the structure in half from its summit to its foundation.

Meaning: Restructuring. Destruction of the old in order to rebuild the new. Demolition of outmoded beliefs. Sudden involuntary illumination. Dramatic realization. Remodeling of obsolete or outdated ideas. Ambition, courage, fighting, combat, strife, war, disruption, adversity, sudden unexpected change. (*Reversed*) Ruin, destruction, disaster, loss, danger, tyranny, oppression. Imprisonment. Bankruptcy. Catastrophe.

17. The Star: Siduri

Siduri (sometimes called *Sabitum* or "the one from Sabu") is the goddess of brewing. She is also a sea goddess and the proprietress of an ale-house. The ale-house served as her palace at the edge of the vast ocean, the Waters of Death, beyond which is the Land of Life where the immortal Utnapishtim lives. She is considered a manifestation of Ishtar, as well as a goddess of wisdom.

The *Epic of Gilgamesh* describes the hero's encounter with Siduri at the edge of the world. Gilgamesh explains his grief over the death of Enkidu and his own search for eternal life. The wise goddess comforts him and tries to guide him into accepting his own mortal limitations. Seeing that Gilgamesh is determined, however, she tells him where to find the ferryman Urshanabi, who can take him across the great sea to find Utnapishtim and possibly find the secret of immortality. Siduri gives Gilgamesh the hope that he needs to continue on his journey.

The card of The Star is attributed to the sign of Aquarius. It shows the goddess Siduri at the edge of the vast ocean. She holds a *hegallu* vase of abundance, from which issue streams of water containing fish, symbols of fertility and plenty. As the goddess of brewing, she is skilled at the arts of fermentation and chemical change. Hanging in the night sky above the goddess is a large star, the disk of the planet Venus. Next to the star are seven dots, the symbol of the *Sebittu* or "Seven" beneficent gods associated with the Pleiades.[26]

Meaning: Meditation, Hope. Insight. Listening to the Inner Voice. Contemplation. Assurance, faith, unexpected help. Inspiration. Enlightenment. Illumination. A gift from the Divine. Fulfillment. Horizons are widened. (*Reversed*) Deceived hope, fantasy. Pessimism. Doubt. Frustration. Disappointment.

18. The Moon: Sin

Unlike the later pantheons of the Greeks and Romans, the older civilizations of Mesopotamia and Egypt conceived of the moon as a male god. *Sin* or *Su'en* (Sumerian *Nannar*) was the god of the moon and chief among the astral triad of gods which included his children Shamash and Ishtar. The Mesopotamians envisioned the day, illumined by the sun, as having been born out of the darkness of the moonlit night, ruled by Sin. Because of this they considered the sun god Shamash as the son of the moon. While the sunlight provided heat, fertility, and food, moonlight served more as a spiritual guide to humanity because of the regularity of its changes. The moon was thereby connected to both celestial and chthonic forces. Nighttime was also the time for lovemaking, and thus Ishtar, the Venusian goddess of love was considered a child of the lunar god.

Sin was the firstborn son of Ellil and Ninlil. The lunar god was known as "he whose deep heart no god can penetrate" because of his mysterious transformation during the moon's various phases. The full moon was his crown, and thus he became known as "the lord of the diadem," "prince of the gods," "the one that furnishes light," "heifer of Anu," "the shining boat of heaven," and "illuminator." Other names associated with the moon god include *Asimbabbar, Namrasit* ("who shines forth"), and *Inbu* ("the fruit" which may refer to the moon's phases). Sin's wife was *Ningal* (or *Nikkal*) the "great lady" and goddess of divination, insight, and dream interpretation.

The following is from a prayer to Sin on the fearful occasion of a lunar eclipse, which the ancients considered a bad omen:

O Sin! O Nannar! Mighty one . . .
O Sin, who art unique, thou brightenest . . .
That giveth light unto the nations . . .
That unto the black-headed race[27] art favorable . . .
Bright is thy light, in heaven . . .
Brilliant is thy torch, like the Fire-god!
Thy brightness fills the broad earth!
The brightness of the nation he gathers, in thy sight . . .
O Anu of the sky, whose purpose no man learns![28]

Like his son Shamash, Sin is considered a god who sees all and dispenses justice. The light provided by the moon at night was a benefit to humans—it guarded against evil night spirits as well as criminals who thrived under the cloak of darkness.

Sin was said to rest in the underworld every month, where he decreed the fate of the deceased. He was also the ruler of time, since the phases of the moon gave humanity and awareness of time and eternity. It was from Sin that the Babylonians cultivated the ideas of past, present, and future. The lunar cycle also suggested the natural cycle of birth, growth, decay, and death. The moon god ruled over the night sky, the lunar calendar of Mesopotamia, destiny, change, secrets, oaths, tides, and predictions. Though a male deity, he was associated with women, ruling over their monthly cycle. The name of Sin was often written as the cuneiform number

30, indicating the number of days in a lunar month. Major holidays were observed according to the moon's phases.

A wise, beneficent, and good-natured god, Sin is sometimes pictured as a mature man with a beard the color of lapis lazuli riding a winged bull. His other sacred animal was the lion-griffin. The crescent moon was his boat which navigated the night sky. But the crescent moon also represented the horns of a bull, alluding to the god's connection with the fertility of livestock. The lunar god was sometimes depicted wearing the crescent moon on his head.

The card of The Moon is attributed to Pisces. It depicts a scene from the Epic of Gilgamesh. Grief-stricken after the death of Enkidu, Gilgamesh wanders through the world searching for immortality. At night, he comes to a mountain pass where lions are prowling. For the first time the mighty warrior is afraid. He prays to Sin, the moon god, to keep him safe.

Meaning: Imagination, intuition, insight. Dreams. "Gut" feelings. Unconscious influences and impulses. Repressed ideas and desires. Psychic abilities. Sixth sense. Evolution. (*Reversed*) Personal demons and self-created phantoms. Illusion, error, lying, falsity, deception. Danger. Enemies.

19. The Sun: Shamash

Shamash (Sumerian *Utu*) was the god of the sun and lord of judgment, truth, and justice. He was the son of the moon god Sin and twin brother of the goddess Ishtar, although some traditions describe him as the son of Anu or of Ellil. Shamash is the older brother of Adad, the weather god. His companion was the goddess *Aya*. Every morning he rose from the gates of the eastern mountains of heaven with the solar rays radiating from his shoulders. Each night he entered the underworld through a gated mountain in the west.

Shamash represents the brilliant sunlight which illuminated the life of man, gave warmth, and caused plants to flourish. He gives light, life, and blessings to all things, and upon him depends the fertility of the land as well as the welfare of humanity. By virtue of his penetrating light which banishes all darkness, Shamash "the one from whom no secrets are hid," is able to see all things. Because of this ability, he is the supreme arbiter of justice, who rewards the virtuous and punishes the wicked. The sun god governed laws, oracles, courage, victory, vitality, truth, moral force, judgment, and retribution. He was also a warrior and a protector of the righteous, and the destroyer of evil. Shamash is attended by two minor deities who are also his children: his daughter *Misaru*, "justice" and his son *Kittu*, "righteousness." In short, Shamash is a "law and order" god, but a compassionate one who upholds the spirit of the law. His favor bestows stability and order, while his anger can bring punishment and devastation.

Shamash's titles include "illuminator of the regions," "lord of living creatures," "king of judgment," and "god of the day." Shamash plays an important role in the lives of humans and this is reflected in the number of stories that he appears in: He is the patron god of Gilgamesh who helps the hero defeat Humbaba. He helps Tammuz escape from the galla damons who seek to carry him off to the underworld. He acts as an advisor in the Story of Etana and the Eagle.

The sun god is sometimes depicted standing in a chariot pulled by horses. At other times he is portrayed standing on a horse, and sometimes he is simply shown striding through the mountain pass. He is often portrayed with the Rod and Ring symbols of justice in his right hand, or shown with a pruning-saw for cutting plants. His primary symbol is the solar disk, an emblem containing a four-pointed star with radiating beams of light.

One of the most beautiful pieces of Mesopotamian liturgy ever written was the Great Hymn to Shamash:

> You climb to the mountains surveying the earth,
> You suspend from the heavens the circle of the lands.
> You care for all the peoples of the lands,
> And everything that Ea, king of the counsellors, had created is entrusted to you.
> Whatever has breath you shepherd without exception,
> You are their keeper in upper and lower regions.
> Regularly and without cease you traverse the heavens,
> Every day you pass over the broad earth. . . .
> Shepherd of that beneath, keeper of that above,
> You, Shamash, direct, you are the light of everything. [. . .]

You observe, Shamash, prayer, supplication, and benediction,
Obeisance, kneeling, ritual murmurs, and prostration.
The feeble man calls you from the hollow of his mouth,
The humble, the weak, the afflicted, the poor, [. . .]
You deliver people surrounded by mighty waves,
In return you receive their pure, clear libations. . . .
They in their reverence laud the mention of you,
And worship your majesty for ever. . . .
Which are the mountains not clothed with your beams?
Which are the regions not warmed
by the brightness of your light?
Brightener of gloom, illuminator of darkness,
Dispeller of darkness, illuminator of the broad earth.[29]

Here Shamash is shown with the solar disk rising up between
the two peaks of the eastern mountains. Rays of light em-
anate from his shoulders and he holds his implement, the
pruning saw. The sun god stands upon his totem animal, the
horse.

Meaning: Glory and honors. Gain, riches, triumph, happiness, joy, pleasure. Birth and renewal. Vindication of daring ideas. Achievement against the odds. The power of
knowledge. Increased perception. Knowledge. Conscious
mind. Spiritual communication. (*Reversed*) Misjudgment.
Vanity, arrogance, showing off.

20. Judgment: Etana and the Eagle

The *Epic of Etana* opens with the search for a king in the city of Kish. The sky god Ellil chooses *Etana* for kingship. The only problem is that Etana has no son who would become heir to the throne.

Meanwhile, in a poplar tree that grows in the shade of Adad's throne, two creatures built their homes—an eagle in the tree's summit and a serpent at its base. The two creatures vie for prey until they decide to become friends, work together, and share their prey. In the presence of Shamash, the solar god of judgment, the eagle and the snake swear their oath of friendship to each other.

This amicable arrangement works for a while, until one day the eagle decides to break his oath and eat the serpent's young when the snake is away. Later, when the serpent returns and finds its children and the eagle gone, it cries out to Shamash for justice. Shamash tells the snake to hide in the carcass of a wild bull and wait for the eagle to come down and feed. The serpent does as the sun god says, and when the eagle crawls inside the carcass to get at the meat, the snake grabs it by the wing, tears its wing-feathers off, and casts the wounded eagle into a pit to die of hunger and thirst.

Broken, the eagle cries out to Shamash to save his life. Shamash scolds the eagle for breaking his oath and committing a wicked act. In disgust Shamash declines to rescue the eagle himself; however, he has compassion, so he tells the bird that someone else will soon come along to help him.

Meanwhile, Etana prays every day to Shamash to be given the "plant of birth" which will enable him to produce a son and heir. The sun god tells Etana to journey along a mountain pass until he comes to the pit where the eagle is trapped. Shamash tells Etana that the eagle will show him where to find the "birth plant."

Etana finds the wounded eagle in the pit and he begins to nurse the creature back to health. After eight months the eagle is well enough to fly again. Grateful, the eagle promises to help Etana find the desired plant. Etana climbs on the eagle's back and together they ascend into the sky to find the goddess Ishtar who alone controls the "birth plant."

As they soar into sky three miles above the earth, Etana becomes frightened and asks the eagle to land. The pair returns to the city of Kish, where Etana has a series of dreams that encourage him to try again and reach heaven. Etana climbs on the back of the Eagle and they take off a second time.

The rest of the story is missing after this point. However, the Sumerian King-list informs us that King Etana of Kish was succeeded by his son Balih. The implication is that Etana and the eagle succeeded in finding the birth-giving plant.

The eagle was judged and punished for his crime, while Etana was given the time-consuming task of rehabilitating the bird. Eventually, Shamash's judgment decided two things —that the eagle had served out his punishment and had learned his lesson, and that Etana's patient care of the bird made him a good candidate for a king. Shamash's judgment also made it possible for Etana's prayers to be answered.

The card of Judgment is attributed to both Fire and Spirit. It shows Etana and the eagle rising up out of the pit.

Shamash, the god of judgment is seen in his solar disk in a heavenly shrine.

Meaning: Final decision, judgment, verdict, resolution, decree, result, outcome, determination of a matter. Settlement. Positive news or announcement. Initiation. Awakening. Spiritual awareness. Change in consciousness. Consecration. Baptism of Fire. Infusion of Divine energy. A new phase. Rebirth and renewal. (*Reversed*) Postponement. Delay. No clear decision or outcome. Punishment. Sentence. Reparations, restitution.

21. The Universe: Anki

The name *Anki* is an amalgamation of two deities, *An* (Anu) the sky god, and *Ki* (Aruru). The literal meaning of *An* and *Ki* is "heaven" and "earth." According to the Eridu version of Creation, An and Ki were born from Nammu, the primordial goddess of the sea. Siblings and lovers, the pair were inseparable while still in their mother's womb and just as inseparable after they were born. They were not An and Ki (heaven *and* earth), but Anki (heaven-earth), one single divine being. From their union was born Ellil, the god of air, who separated his two parents. An took the heaven for his abode, Ki took the earth for her home, and Ellil ruled the air that rested between them. Thus was the universe created.

The card of the Universe is attributed to both Saturn and the element of earth. It shows Anki, the two deities joined as one—the archetypal sky father and earth mother united as one force. Between them is an ancient circular map of the world from the viewpoint of the Babylonians—complete with rivers, mountains, and cities represented as geometric shapes and circles.

Surrounding Anki is a creature from another Creation Epic, *Enuma Elish*. The body of Tiamat the chaos dragon has been split into two halves by Marduk—the upper half to create the celestial world, and the lower half to create the terrestrial earth. Beyond the outer shell of the dragon is the starry heavens.

Meaning: Successful completion, conclusion, culmination. Total unity. Closure. Synthesis, Reward, acclaim, triumph.

Truth and honesty. Movement, travel. Cosmic consciousness. Investigation into the subconscious. The keys to the
kingdom. Coming full circle. The ending of one phase
and the beginning of another. A new cycle of growth and
experience is about to begin. (*Reversed*) Stagnation, end-
less delay, loss of momentum. Indolence, apathy. Lessons
not learned. Fear of change. Payback.

---

1. Genesis 1:2.

2. King, Leonard W., *The Seven Tablets of Creation*, 3.

3. I have used "reversed" throughout this book to mean inverted, nega-
tively placed, or ill-dignified cards (surrounded with negative cards),
depending upon the reader's preference.

4. Smith, George, *The Chaldean Account of Genesis*, 200–202.

5. Jastrow, Morris, *The Religion of Babylonia and Assyria*, 137.

6. Anuna or Annuna (Anunnakku). Possible meaning: "princely offspring." A generic word for "the gods," particularly the earliest gods
who were born first and not distinguished from one another with individual names. Later the Anuna gods came to be defined as gods of
the earth or chthonic deities.

7. Bottéro, Jean, *Religion in Ancient Mesopotamia*, 139–140.

8. Or *Beltu*, a title Ishtar shares with Sarpanitu, the wife of Marduk.

9. The Igigi or Igigu gods were considered the "great gods" of heaven. A
term for celestial deities.

10. Bottéro, Jean, *Religion in Ancient Mesopotamia*, 145–146.

11. King, Leonard W., *Babylonian Magic and Sorcery*, 26–27.

12. Translation by E. A. Speiser in *Ancient Near Eastern Texts Relating to the
Old Testament*, 3rd edition, edited by James Pritchard (Princeton, 1969),
60–72.

13. King, Leonard W., *The Seven Tablets of Creation*, 111.

14. Pinches, Theophilus, *The Religion of Babylonia and Assyria* (Project Gutenburg).

15. Bottéro, Jean, *Religion in Ancient Mesopotamia*, 57.

16. King, Leonard W., *Babylonian Magic and Sorcery*, 84.

17. Spence, Lewis, *Myths and Legends of Babylonia & Assyria*, 126–127.

18. Kramer, Samuel, *The Sacred Marriage Rite: Aspects of Faith, Myth, and Ritual in Ancient Sumer*, 77.

19. Ibid.

20. Over time it became clear that the Akkadian Adad and the Canaanite Ba'al were two separate deities.

21. Spence, *Myths and Legends of Babylonia & Assyria*, 218.

22. Kovacs, M. G. (trans.), *The Epic of Gilgamesh*, 4.

23. Kramer, Samuel, *The Sumerians: Their History, Culture, and Character*, 124.

24. Ibid., 125.

25. Wolkstein, Diane, and Samel Noah Kramer, *Inanna, Queen of Heaven and Earth*, 84.

26. These Seven gods were often invoked in magical incantations to combat evil spirits. These are not to be confused with the "Seven" demons who acted as Erra's assistants.

27. The Sumerians referred to themselves as the "black-headed ones."

28. King, Leonard W., *Babylonian Magic and Sorcery*, 5.

29. Lambert, W. G., *Babylonian Wisdom Literature*, 127.

— The Wands —

The Ace of Wands: Natural Force

The wand represented in this card surrounded by an aura of flames is the double lion-headed scepter of the goddess Ishtar, whose sacred animal is the lion. Lions were common throughout Mesopotamia and were featured motifs in Babylonian art. They were usually depicted with bared teeth, and their fearsome strength made them a popular symbol for warrior deities such as Ishtar and Erra. However, the Mesopotamians thought of lions as canines rather than felines, which accounts for the Akkadian name for the constellation of Leo meaning "the Great Dog."

The symbolism of the lion, long associated with heat and flame, is also used to indicate the fire element of the Ace of Wands. It is a scepter of great power. Beneath the wand is the cuneiform symbol for the number one.

Meaning: Force, strength, power, energy, inspiration, innovation, conception. A good time to start a new project. Birth. An auspicious new beginning. (*Reversed*) Failure of a new project. False start.

The Two of Wands: Dominion

The card shows two ram-headed scepters. This particular implement is the wand of Ea, the god of magic and incantation. These wands also allude to the astrological influence of Aries. The Babylonians viewed the stars and constellations as celestial reflections of pastoral flocks of sheep, grazing in the night sky.

On the bottom right of the card is the symbol of the rod and ring, an emblem of high divinity and justice. On the left is the cuneiform numeral two.

Meaning: Strength of will. Influence over others, authority, power, dominion. Energy, restlessness, and optimism. Looking forward to new things. Responsible use of power. (*Reversed*) Success may be accompanied by boredom. Sudden, unexpected change. Sudden anger and ferocity. Blind ambition with no regard for others.

The Three of Wands: Achievement

Here we see the hero Gilgamesh at the end of his journey. He has accepted the fact that epic deeds will not make him immortal—it is his city of Uruk that will live on and ensure the civilization of humanity. It is to Uruk that Gilgamesh has now returned, to act as a reliable king and secure the vitality of the city. He stops to marvel at his highest achievement:

> He came to a far road, was weary, found peace,
> and set all his labours on a tablet of stone.
> He built the rampart of Uruk-the-Sheepfold,
> of holy Eanna, the sacred storehouse.
> See its wall like a strand of wool,
> View its parapet that none could copy!
> Take the stairway of a bygone era,
> Draw near to Eanna. The seat of Ishtar the goddess,
> That no later king could ever copy!
> Climb Uruk's wall and walk back and forth!
> Survey its foundations, examine the brickwork!
> Were its bricks not fired in an oven?
> Did the Seven Sages not lay its foundations?[1]

In the final twelve-tablet version of the epic, Gilgamesh does manage to become immortal, but only by becoming an underworld god—not as a human being.

In this card, Gilgamesh stands on a hill overlooking the city of Uruk admiring his great and gleaming city and finally at peace with himself after his long arduous journey. The solar disk graces the blue sky above the city, and three ram-headed wands crossed in peace and turned outward fill the top of the card. Above the hero is the cuneiform numeral three.

Meaning: Success. Realization of hope. Completion of labor, success of the struggle. Building on one's strengths. Peace of mind. Contentment. Cooperation from others. (*Reversed*) Disturbing memories. Disappointments. Isolation. Retreat into fantasy. Self-absorbed and impractical.

The Four of Wands: Reward

While digging at several sites in ancient Sumer, archeologists discovered a number of figurines in reverential poses, with large staring eyes made of lapis lazuli. Votive statues of such figures were often left in Sumerian temples so that the deity of the temple would never be without an adoring audience of the respectful humans that the figures represented. Inscriptions on the statues indicate that they were created to act as pious substitutes for live worshipers. The message on one such statue reads "It offers prayers," while another says, "Statue, say to my lord . . ." It was the hope of Sumerian worshipers that by leaving such consecrated figurines in the temple of a god, their continuous devotion would be rewarded by the god's blessings. Constant attention to one's personal deity was thought to result in the attainment of a good life:

> Every day worship your god.
> Sacrifice and benediction are the
> Proper accompaniment of incense.
> Present your free-will offering to your god.
> For this is proper toward the gods.
> Prayer, supplication, and prostration
> Offer him daily, and you will get your reward.[2]

Their purpose indicates that these loyal, sculpted surrogates bear a similarity to the mummy-wrapped *ushabti* figures found in Egyptian tombs.

Here we see the figurines of four worshipers, hands held in an attitude of prayer. They stare wide-eyed at the heavens anticipating that their ardent devotion will be rewarded. Above the figures are two ram-headed wands and two Venus-disk wands. The wands are upright and balanced. In the center is the cuneiform numeral four.

Meaning: Optimism, compensation, success. Harmony, prosperity and comfort. Stability. Haven or refuge. (*Reversed*) Success that is not apparent. Too conventional or reliant on tradition.

The Five of Wands: Conflict

The average Mesopotamian saw the world around him full of supernatural forces: gods, demigods, and spirits. The gods came to symbolize supernatural forces that were personalized—given anthropomorphic form, expression, motivation, and emotion. But there were other spiritual forces that were not so humanized. Of the demons or spirits, some were considered good and others evil. Such spirits were often depicted as human-animal hybrid creatures. The darker demonic forces were considered harmful and irrational in their actions; however, in many cases they were simply seen as administrators of the gods—their destructive activities were assumed to be the carrying out of divine punishment. Some spirits even had rivalries with other spirits and were considered mortal enemies.

This card shows an Assyrian lion-centaur, a creature with the body and legs of a lion and the torso of a man who wears the horned crown of divinity. The name of this entity is *Urmahlullû* or the "lion-man." Images of this creature were placed outside ablution rooms for protection. Here he is seen battling against the demon *Mukil-res-lemutii* or "evil attendant" who takes the form of a lion. At the top of the card are five lion-headed wands, symbols of the war god Erra. The lion-heads on the wands are placed in opposition to each other. On the left is the cuneiform numeral five.

Meaning: Quarreling and fighting. Strife, struggle, conflict, confrontation. Upheaval. May indicate healthy competition. (*Reversed*) Cruelty and viciousness. An unfair battle. Expect a dishonest and dirty fight. Legal disputes.

The Six of Wands: Victory

In this card we see a priest wearing the ritual costume of the god *La-tarak,* a lion-headed figure dressed in the pelt of a lion. La-tarak was a god who guarded doorways and protected the devout against sorcery and evil magic. Babylonian art provides many examples of what appear to be animal parts (lion pelts, fish skins, bird wings) used as costumes in ritual ceremonies.

One religious figure who may have dressed in the lionskin of La-tarak for the power that it imparted was the exorcist or *Asipu,* one of the most important members of clergy. It was the job of the exorcist to cast out the "evil" that was thought to be the cause of all illness and misfortune. The priest-exorcist was skilled in diagnosing the ills of the afflicted—he had to be at the same time a reader of omens, a psychoanalyst, a physician, an insightful councilor, and a skilled ritualist. Once the exorcist determined the appropriate ritual formula for the situation, he officiated over all aspects of the ceremony, including the gathering of all needed items and materials. He performed several purification ceremonies. He recited numerous invocations to the gods—spells that granted the exorcist divine authority, victory over evil, and the power to heal the patient. He instructed the patient to recite certain portions of invocations. He also provided the patient with follow-up advice, ointments, poultices, and protective amulets.

In this card the hands of the lion-garbed priest are held in a gesture of prayer and supplication. The figure invokes the god La-tarak. He identifies himself as having been commissioned by the god to act on his behalf. The powers granted to him by the god ensure his victory over evil. Six wands, two with lion heads, are shown on the left, crossed in victory and peace. Above the priest is the cuneiform numeral six.

Meaning: Gain, victory after strife, success gained by labor, triumph through perseverance. Public recognition and honor. Arrival of good news. A turning point for the better. Advancement in the arts and sciences. (*Reversed*) News delayed. False optimism that leads to weakness. Pessimism. Pride and insolence.

The Seven of Wands: Courage

This card shows the descent of the goddess Ishtar into the underworld to face her sister, Ereshkigal, the goddess of death. Although Ishtar had knowledge of all the heavens, she had no knowledge of the underworld, and was determined to obtain this information. The daring goddess resolves to enter the underworld:

> To the land of no return, the land of darkness,
> Ishtar, the daughter of Sin directed her thought,
> Directed her thought, Ishtar, the daughter of Sin,
> To the house of shadows, the dwelling, of Irkalla,
> To the house without exit for him who enters therein,
> To the road, whence there is no turning,[. . .]
> Ishtar on arriving at the gate of the land of no return,
> To the gatekeeper thus addressed herself:
> "Gatekeeper, ho, open thy gate!
> Open thy gate that I may enter!
> If thou openest not the gate to let me enter,
> I will break the door, I will wrench the lock,
> I will smash the door-posts, I will force the doors."[3]

Ishtar threatens to make the dead outnumber the living if she is not allowed to enter. The gatekeeper lets her pass and she descends to the underworld to confront her dark sister. At seven doors along the way, Ishtar finds herself being stripped of her clothing and jewels, until at length she stands naked before the enraged Ereshkigal, who promptly has her killed. At the death of Ishtar, all fertility on earth ceases—no plants blossom and no animals can give birth. The gods become distressed at this situation. The wise god Ea sends an envoy to secure Ishtar's release and restore her with the Waters of Life. In anger, Ereshkigal demands a substitute who will take Ishtar's place in the underworld. Ishtar's lover Tammuz, who showed no emotion at his mate's disappearance is chosen.

Here we see the intrepid Ishtar boldly descending the steps leading to Ereshkigal's chamber. Seven wands are shown on the upper left. The wands are crossed but unbalanced. The single lion-headed wand is shown apart from the rest, indicating that in times of trial, one is often alone. Below the goddess Ishtar is the cuneiform numeral seven.

Meaning: Courage in the face of opposition and difficulty. Victory that depends on energy and determination. Triumph through valor. Obstacles can be overcome through sustained effort. May indicate a good time to tackle a risky venture. (*Reversed*) Hesitation and indecision leads to defeat or loss of opportunity. Depression, anxiety, embarrassment.

The Eight of Wands: Swift Action

This card shows the god *Usmû* (Sumerian *Isimud*) who functions as a messenger for Ea, the god of wisdom. Like the Roman god Janus, Usmû has two faces which look in opposite directions. His name means "with two faces."

In the ancient world a professional messenger was known as a *mar shipri* or "son of the message." These messengers played an important role in Mesopotamia where a swift, reliable system of communication was essential to the security and well-being of the kingdom. The mar shipri carried a bag around his neck containing tablets of communications between kings and regional governors. He traveled along "royal roads"—major routes of commerce throughout the empire dotted every twenty or thirty miles with armed outposts.

This card shows the double-featured Usmû. With one face turned toward his lord Ea, and the other toward the recipient of the divine communication, Usmû was a swift messenger. The position of the wands are meant to convey rapid movement. To the left of the god are eight wands, while above him is the cuneiform numeral eight.

Meaning: Swiftness, rapidity, and movement. Great speed. Ending of delays means renewed activity. Time to take decisive action. Hopeful change. News, communications, travel. (*Reversed*) Swift energy that dissipates too quickly to be effective. Wasted energy. Jealousy and quarrels.

The Nine of Wands: Power

The subject here is the hero Gilgamesh as described in Tablet V of the epic. Gilgamesh and Enkidu resolve to kill *Humbaba*, a powerful monster appointed as guardian of the Cedar Forest by the god Ellil. Humbaba, protected by seven layers of fear-inspiring radiance, was described as a giant with lion's claws and a horrible face. The two heroes attack Humbaba, aided by the sun god Shamash who assaults the monster with ferocious winds. Humbaba pleads for his life but Enkidu argues that the monster must die, and so Gilgamesh kills him. The heroes then chop down cedar trees, choosing one particular tree to serve as lumber for a new door to Ellil's temple in Uruk. Then Gilgamesh cuts off the head of Humbaba for a trophy.

This card shows a valiant Gilgamesh holding the severed head of the monster Humbaba. Although victorious he bears wounds from the battle on his right arm and leg. Nine wands are above him, three of which are crossed in power and victory, while the other six are upright and balanced. On the lower right of the card is the cuneiform numeral nine.

Meaning: Tremendous strength and stability that is unassailable. Self-discipline. Daring in defense and victory in attack. Great success after a period of strife. Battle-tested. Recovery from illness. Seeking justice and fairness. (*Reversed*) Defensiveness. Battle-scarred. Adversity, obstacles, and delay.

The Ten of Wands: Oppression

As stated in the section describing the Five of Wands, the Babylonians believed in a world fully populated with deities and spirits. There were many species of spirits or demons, some of which were good and beneficial, while others were evil and harmful to humans. Many magical incantations and exorcisms included the idea of banishing evil spirits and invoking good ones, such as in the following spell to combat illness in a man:

> *May the wicked demons depart! [. . .]*
> *The favourable demon, the favorable giant,*
> *May they penetrate into his body.*[4]

Evil demons, though feared, were not always considered responsible for their harmful actions—oftentimes they were considered as agents who simply carried out the will of the gods. And as in the case of the creatures *Urmahlullû* and *Mukil-res-lemutii* shown in the fifth card of this suit, some spirits were considered deadly enemies of other spirits. Because of such supernatural rivalries, the Babylonians believed that one demon could be invoked to combat the evil acts of another demon.

This card shows the demon *Pazuzu*, king of the evil wind demons, said to be the son of the god Hanbi. He is depicted as a winged creature with a canine face, large bulging eyes, scaly skin, a serpent-headed penis, and the claws of an eagle. Although he was considered evil, Pazuzu was sometimes employed for beneficent proposes, such as protection against foul and harmful winds, particularly the west wind. His arch-enemy was Lamastu (see The Devil), killer of unborn and newborn children. To counter this malevolent goddess and force her back into the underworld, statutes of Pazuzu were placed around the houses of pregnant women, who often wore amulets in the form of Pazuzu's head.

Meaning: Overburdened and oppressed. Imprisoned. Taking on too many responsibilities. Having to choose your battles due to overextension of resources. Having to choose between the lesser of two evils. (*Reversed*) Cruelty malice, treachery, revenge, injustice. Selfishness. Burdens are increased.

The Kerub of Wands: Lion-headed Spirit

The card shows a winged, lion-headed spirit with upright ears, the head of a lion, the torso of a man, and the feet of a bird. He wears a short kilt and carries a club-like wand.

In the Neo-Assyrian and Neo-Babylonian periods, this type of spirit was known as the *ugallu*, or "big weather-creature," and was regarded as a fierce but beneficent spirit who guarded against evil demons and illnesses. Like other Kerubic creatures, statuettes of ugallu spirits were ceremonially placed in houses or buried in the foundations of buildings for protection.

Meaning: Divine aid and protection. Divine Intervention. Inspiration and innovation. (*Reversed*) Divine intervention is not forthcoming. Lack of inspiration.

The King of Wands: Nusku

This card shows *Nusku*, who was considered a god of light and the sacred ritual fire, as well as a son and high official of Ellil. (In some traditions he was the son of Sin, the Moon god.) Titles of Nusku include: "wise prince, the flame of heaven," "he whose clothing is splendour," "the forceful fire-god," "exalter of the mountain peaks," and "uplifter of the torch, the enlightener of darkness." Nusku was regularly invoked in magical incantations designed to burn sorcerers and black magicians so that they would no longer cause harm. His symbol was the oil lamp, and he manifested himself in the sacrificial flame of the temple—consuming offerings and sending clouds of sweet incense to the great gods above.

Praised as the "lofty one" among the gods, Nusku's command is total and absolute. He is the great messenger of the gods as well as their chief counselor. The god is clothed in splendor, radiating an unquenchable light. He has numerous other attributes, all underscoring his dignity, power, brilliance, and the awe that he is able to inspire in humans.

The reference to the indispensable presence of the fire-god in the temple is rather interesting. Sacrifice always entailed the use of fire. To whatever deity the offering was made, Gibil-Nusku could not in any case be overlooked. The fire constituted the medium, as it were, between the worshipper and the deity addressed. The fire-god is in truth the messenger who carries the sacrifice into the presence of the god worshipped. Even Shamash, though himself personifying fire, is forced to acknowledge the power of Gibil-Nusku, who, we are told elsewhere, is invoked, even when sacrifices are made to the sun-god.[5]

Here Nuska is shown emerging from the smoke of incense which rises from three oil lamps at the bottom of the card. Above the lamps is a double-headed wand.

Meaning: Dynamic, fiery force that is swift but not lasting. A strong-willed person who is a natural leader and commander. A mature, charismatic man (or person) who is active, energetic generous, brave, ambitious, and spontaneous. (*Reversed*) He may be cruel, brutal, intolerant, and impulsive.

The Queen of Wands: Aya

This card depicts *Aya* (Sumerian *Serida*) a goddess of light who was the consort and "beloved one" of Shamash, the sun god. The marriage of these solar deities was ritually celebrated during the Babylonian New Year Festival beginning on the Vernal Equinox in the ancient month of Nisan. Because of the sun's life-giving energy, Aya is associated with fertility and sexual love.

Aya is credited with receiving the sun upon his setting in the west, leading some to speculate that she represented the "double sun" from the magnified solar disk that can be seen at sunset.

Here the goddess is shown wearing the horned cap of divinity, crowned with the sun's golden rays. A double-headed wand is shown on the right.

Meaning: Steady, creative force that is not as swift as it is lasting. A woman (or person) of authority who is self-assertive, self-confident, and talented. She is honest, sincere, good-natured, animated, and magnetic. She is adaptable and steady, with great power to attract and command. (*Reversed*) She may be jealous, deceitful, bitter, vengeful, and domineering.

The Prince of Wands: Girra

This card portrays the god *Girra* (Sumerian *Gibil*), who represented deified fire. This god, the son of Anu and Sala (or Ki), symbolized every aspect of fire—the destructive force of fire epitomized by the oppressive heat of the Mesopotamian summer, as well as the creative force of fire used in the potter's kiln, the baker's oven, and the metal worker's forge. Because of fire's many useful qualities, Girra was known as "the founder of cities."

Fire was considered a great counterforce against malevolent magic and sorcery, and thus Girra, like Nusku, was a deity regularly called upon to burn evil magicians. In a ceremony, the bewitched individual would raise a lighted torch in one hand and repeat the invocation recited by the priest-exorcist. Oftentimes the incantation was recited in a whisper, to correspond to the soft tones in which spirits were thought to convey their messages.

In this card Girra is shown holding a scepter and standing in the middle of an ethereal circle of incantation. Surrounded by a ring of flames, his demeanor is stern and unyielding.

Meaning: A force that is swift and lasting although not especially strong or stable. A young man (or person) who is confident, energetic, intelligent, talented, witty, impulsive, and passionate. (*Reversed*) He may be over-confident, insensitive, reckless, intolerant, and cruel.

The Princess of Wands: Sarpanitu

The goddess *Sarpanitu* was the wife of the great god Marduk and principle goddess of the city of Babylon. Since her husband Marduk was often called *Bel* or "lord," she acquired the feminine tile *Belit* meaning "lady." Under the name *Erua* she was worshiped as a goddess of pregnancy and childbirth (from the Akkadian word *eru*, "to be pregnant"). One of her special functions was to protect the unborn progeny. Because of her special function, Sarpanitu was said to have knowledge that was concealed from men.

At one time Assyro-Babylonian scholars thought her name meant "she who shines like refined silver," although scholars today think it means "she of Sarpan," perhaps referring to a village near Babylon. The priests of Babylon gave her the title of "seed-producing goddess," to affirm her connection to Marduk, the god responsible for the renewal of spring. The divine couple was lavishly praised during the great festival of the New Year.

In this card Sarpanitu is shown heavy with child as an indication of her divine function of giving birth. Her face is shown enlarged on the right side of the card. Below it is a scepter.

Meaning: Strong and enduring force. Able to create ideas and manifest them. A young woman (or person) who is brilliant, courageous, adventurous, enthusiastic, creative, captivating, and vigorous. A person who craves new experience and is full of new ideas. (*Reversed*) Lacks commitment. Superficial. Overly dramatic. Desires power. Sudden to love, anger, or revenge. May be unstable, irrational, domineering, cruel, and unforgiving.

1. George, Andrew, *The Epic of Gilgamesh: The Babylonian Epic Poem and Other Texts in Akkadian and Sumerian,* 1–2.

2. Bottéro, 165.

3. Jastrow, Morris, *The Civilization of Babylonia and Assyria.*

4. Lenormant, Francois, *Chaldean Magic: Its Origin and Development,* 11.

5. Jastrow, Morris, *The Religion of Babylonia and Assyria,* 279. Although acknowledging that Gibil (Girra) and Nusku are separate deities, he treats them together under the double designation of Gibil-Nusku.

— The Cups —

The Ace of Cups: Fertility

The cup represented in this card is based upon a famous steatite vase or libation vessel carved with dragons and entwined snakes. The vase is inscribed with a dedication by Prince Gudea of Lagash to his personal protective deity, *Ningiszida* ("Lord of the Good Tree"), who presided over the growth and blossoming of trees. The son of Ninazu, Ningiszida was an underworld guardian whose symbol was the horned serpent or *basmu*. Prince Gudea called him "the Throne-bearer of the Earth." The Mesopotamians perceived a similarity between a swift-flowing river and the smooth gliding motion of a serpent. Astrologically, Ningiszida is associated with the constellation of Hydra, the Water Snake.

Stylized waves of water are seen beneath the cup, while above the cup is an inverted triangle. At the bottom of the card is the number one, written in cuneiform as a single wedge.

Meaning: Abundance in all things. Fertility, beauty, happiness. New pleasure. The beginning of love, consummation of a union, celebration, joy, spiritual nourishment. (*Reversed*) Instability, Disruption, bareness, dishonesty, infidelity, disappointment. Loss of Faith.

The Two of Cups: Love

This card shows two Neo-Assyrian rhytons or luxurious drinking vessels, one made of silver, the other of gold. The base of the gold rhyton is fashioned to look like the head and torso of a lion, while the silver one is shaped like the head and fore-quarters of an antelope. Beside each vessel is a hand, while in the center of the card is the cuneiform numeral two.

The gold and silver vessels are meant to portray the archetypal masculine and feminine energies in perfect balance and harmony. The hands, one feminine and pale, the other masculine and dark, also point to the union of opposites.

Meaning: Masculine and feminine united. Romance. Natural love. Spiritual union. Marriage, friendship, partnership, harmony. (*Reversed*) End of a relationship, infidelity, jealousy, deceit.

The Three of Cups: Abundance

In this card we see the figure of a man carrying a basket full of fruit. Above him are three vases with streams of water issuing from their mouths. This type of short-necked, round-bodied, flared rim vessel is known as the "flowing vase" or "fertility vase." A common motif in Mesopotamian art, the name of this vase was *hegallu*, which means "abundance." It was a symbol of fecundity and plenty. Three stylized trees surround the figure of the man, while above him is the cuneiform numeral three.

Meaning: Plenty, abundance, success, bounty, pleasure, fulfillment, joy, celebration. Maternity. Birth. Healing. Friendship. (*Reversed*) Loss of happiness. Loss of Friendship. Lust without love. Exploitation of one's emotions. Self-indulgence.

The Four of Cups: Mixed Blessing

The subject of this card is taken from the Babylonian epic of *Erra and Ishum*. In this story, the war god Erra is in a state of depression. Even his weapons grumble about being kept in storage to gather dust. Babylon is in decline—the jewel city is losing its luster due to the negligence of the elderly god Marduk, who has become disengaged from the lives of his people. Through boredom and disinterest Marduk has let his marvelous kingdom stagnate. Erra asks him why he has also let his appearance become disheveled. The war god criticizes Marduk for letting his regalia become dirty and his crown tarnished.

Irritated, Marduk goes off to see his tailor, leaving Erra in charge of the city. This proves to be a mistake for the aggressive war god attacks the city, destroying the righteous as well as the wicked. Total destruction of Babylon is prevented by the god Ishum, the wise counselor of Erra, who finally convinces the war god to end the bloodshed. Ishum makes a prediction that, due to Erra's restraint, the Babylonians who survived the ordeal will ultimately prosper and thrive.

In this card we see Marduk facing the other way. He has forgotten his past days of glory and has turned his back on his greatest accomplishments.

Four water vessels are shown, two fluted libation cups, and two ceramic pots. This signifies the idea of mixed blessing or blended fortune. In the center of the four vessels is the cuneiform numeral two.

Meaning: A period of ups and downs, highs and lows. A roller-coaster ride. Boredom, discontent, and disinterest arising from apathy. Numbing routines and habits. (*Reversed*) Overindulgence. New opportunity. New ideas and events.

The Five of Cups: Loss

This card shows a scene from the *Epic of Gilgamesh*. The gods have decided that Enkidu must die as punishment for the killings of Humbaba and the Bull of Heaven. At first Enkidu curses his fate, but then comes to accept the inevitable. Gilgamesh is devastated by the death of his friend. He weeps for Enkidu and begins to fear his own mortality:

> *I wept over him for six days and nights [. . .]*
> *I was afraid of death, and therefore I wander over the country.*
> *The fate of my friend lieth heavily upon me,*
> *Therefore am traveling on a long journey through the country.*
> *[. . .]*
> *How is it possible for me to keep silence?*
> *How is it possible for me to cry out?*
> *My friend whom I loved hath become like the dust.*
> *Enkidu, my friend whom I loved hath become like the dust.*
> *Shall not I myself also be obliged to lay me down*
> *And never again rise up to all eternity?* [1]

Thus began Gilgamesh on his journey across the world in search of eternal life.

This card shows the distraught Gilgamesh overcome by the loss of Enkidu. Five red fluted cups are shown in disarray. In the midst of the cups is a scorpion, and in the upper right is shown the cuneiform numeral five.

Meaning: Disappointment, sorrow, pain, regret. Indicates a need for reassessment. Acceptance of loss. (*Reversed*) Refusal to accept loss. Support from friends during a difficult period. New interests emerge after a disturbing or sad event. New focus on what has *not* been lost.

The Six of Cups: Pleasure

An ample supply of food and drink was seen as one of Mesopotamia's greatest achievements—it provided the means for the building of cities and the various occupations and skills created by an urban civilization. Sacrificial meals offered to the gods were huge banquets that were subsequently consumed by the temple's staff. Eating and drinking were important social activities, not only for the gods, but for those who served them. It was thought that the gods took great delight in these feasts and rewarded those who provided it.

> "Give food to eat, beer to drink,
> Grant what is asked, provide for and honour,
> In this, a man's god take's pleasure."[2]

The pleasure of sex in the ancient world lives on in erotic art of the period, including clay models of couples embracing. Some of these pieces may have been created to symbolize the *hieros gamos* or sacred marriage that ensured the fertility of the land. Love poetry in Mesopotamia was often full of eroticism and passion such as in the song Tammuz sings for Inanna-Ishtar:

> "O Lady, your breast is your field.
> Inanna, your breast is your field.
> Your broad field pours out plants.
> Your broad field pours out grain.
> Water flows from on high for your servant.
> Bread flows from on high for your servant.
> Pour it out for me, Inanna.

I will drink all you offer." ³

This card shows Ashurbanipal, the last great warrior-king of Assyria, reclining and dining with his queen Tashmetum-sharrat. The couple is relaxed and contented. At the top of the card, a man and woman are shown embraced in a kiss. In addition to the six fluted cups, the solar disk and the figure of a scorpion (emblems of the card's astrological decan) are also shown. In the center is the cuneiform numeral six.

Meaning: Happiness built on past efforts. Enjoyment, gratification, indulgence, gain, success, well-being. Sharing. Pleasant memories. Remembering. (*Reversed*) Living in the past. Overly nostalgic. Failure to adapt to new circumstances. Disturbing memories.

The Seven of Cups: Seduction

This card portrays a seductive winged goddess holding the symbols of the rod and ring. The goddess, who has the feet of a bird, wears the horned crown of divinity. She stands upon a pair of lions flanked by owls.

This image of the goddess has often been identified as Lilith, the "dark maid" who, along with the *Anzu* bird took over Inanna's sacred *huluppu* tree until forcibly evicted by Gilgamesh. It is important to point out that Lilith is not a Sumerian or Babylonian goddess. The name Lilith comes from the Akkadian words *lilitu* and *ardat lili*, the name of a class of female storm demons who were dangerous as well as sexually aggressive toward men. They were not considered deities. At some point the lilitu was incorporated into Hebrew legend as Lilith, Adam's first wife, who was eventually transformed into the demonic seductress mentioned in the Hebrew Scriptures.

In recent years, however, the image described above, long thought to be that of Lilith, is now considered by many scholars to be an underworld or sexualized aspect of the goddess Inanna–Ishtar. Aspects of the figure that point to its being a goddess and not a harmful demon include the presence of the divine horned crown, the rod and ring symbols of justice, and the lions which are Ishtar's sacred animal.

Seven fluted cups surround the goddess. Above her left hand is the cuneiform numeral seven.

Meaning: Enticement, temptation, seduction. Overindulgence. Obsession. Too much of a good thing can be bad. Addiction. Daydream, fantasy, illusion, imagination. Escapism. Self-delusion. (*Reversed*) Manifestation of one's dreams. Freedom from addiction or obsession. Determination, resolution.

The Eight of Cups: Neglect

This card shows another scene from the *Epic of Gilgamesh*. After a long and arduous quest, Gilgamesh's journey eventually leads him to his ancestor Utnapishtim (the Mesopotamian Noah). Gilgamesh knows his ancestor has become immortal and he hopes to learn the secret of eternal life. Utnapishtim tells Gilgamesh the story of the Great Flood that destroyed all of humanity except for Utnapishtim and his family. After the flood, the gods made Utnapishtim and his wife immortal, but it was the only time they ever granted eternal life to humans. Gilgamesh could not yet accept the lesson of his own mortality, so Utnapishtim tells him where to find a magical plant that, when eaten, will make Gilgamesh young forever. Gilgamesh dives to the bottom of the sea to fetch the plant.

On the journey back to Uruk, Gilgamesh stops to bathe in a pool of water. As he does so, a snake is attracted to the plant, carries it off, and eats it. Gilgamesh's neglect has resulted in loss of his one chance at eternal youth.

The card shows Gilgamesh swimming in the water, while at the water's edge a snake prepares to carry off the plant of eternal youth. Eight fluted cups slowly sink to the dark bottom of the pond. Below the figure is the cuneiform numeral eight.

Meaning: Success abandoned. Indolence. Things thrown aside as soon as gained. Happiness, security, and stability are deliberately left behind. Disillusion with things that once provided happiness. A quest for growth. (*Reversed*) The time to leave has not yet arrived. Hanging on or clinging to an outmoded situation. Running away rather than facing problems.

The Nine of Cups: Contentment

This card shows a Babylonian "fish-garbed figure" or bearded man wearing the skin of a fish. Images of fish-garbed figures standing over the bed of a sick man are thought to represent priests exorcizing demons of disease. Like the lion-headed and eagle-headed spirits, statuettes of fish-garbed figures were considered magically protective—they were placed in doorways or ritually buried (often in groups of seven) under the floors of houses and other buildings.

Some ancient texts describe the fish-garbed figures as *apkallu* meaning "wise men" or "sages." The Seven Sages were antediluvian beings who lived before the time of the Great Flood. It is said that during the time before the Flood, the wise god Ea sent the Seven Sages, in the form of fish, to teach humanity the arts and sciences of civilization—language, writing, agriculture, and the building of cities. The most well-known of the sages was *Adapa* (also called *Uan* or *Oannes*). According to Berossos,[4] Oannes, an entity who was half man, half fish, swam up to the shore of the Persian Gulf and began to teach the Babylonians all manner of knowledge.

In the story of *Adapa* the main figure is a priest of Ea in the ancient city of Eridu. Adapa is considered to be extremely wise, having been trained in all manner of knowledge by Ea. As a priest he is skilled in the duties of religious observance, performing services that are important to both gods and humans. One of his responsibilities is to prepare food and drink to be offered to the gods. According to the story,

Adapa takes a boat out to sea to catch fish for the offering table of Ea's temple. While he is out on the water a ferocious storm blows up and sinks his vessel. Angry and wet, Adapa utters a curse and instantly breaks the wing of the South Wind. This act infuriates the sky god Anu who orders that the sage be punished.

Concerned, Ea advises Adapa how to behave when he ascends to heaven to stand before Anu. Ea also advises that if Adapa wants to return again to the physical world, he should not eat or drink anything offered by Anu, particularly the bread of death and the water of death. When he reaches the gates of heaven, Adapa flatters the guardians Dumuzi and Gizzida, who speak in his favor to Anu. When asked by Anu to explain the reason for his harsh curse against the South Wind, the sage does so, and Anu is appeased. Adapa is then offered the bread and water of eternal life, which he refuses as per Ea's instructions, and remains mortal. He refuses the gift of immortality because he did not intend to stay in heaven—he is needed by the people on earth. Adapa is content with his earthly life as priest-sage, temple fisherman, and teacher of humanity. He accepts the gifts of a new priestly garment and oil with which to anoint himself, before returning to the physical world to minister to his god and his people.

This card shows the sage Adapa in his fish-garb. He carries a vessel called the *banduddu* or "bucket" in one hand and a fir-tree cone known as the *mullilu* or "purifier" in the other. To the right of the figure are eight cups, while at the top of the card is the cuneiform numeral eight.

Meaning: Complete success, satisfaction, advantage, stability. Perfect happiness. Wish fulfilled. Generosity of spirit. Compassion for others. Kindness and aid toward others. Inner security and peace. Rejection of the superficial. (*Reversed*) Vanity, self-absorption. Conceit. Fault-finding. Disappointments. Foolishness.

The Ten of Cups: Success

This card depicts the boat or ark of *Utnapishtim*, the Mesopotamian Noah, who survived the Great Flood. Utnapishtim has many names, including *Atrahasis* meaning "extra-wise." In the story of Gilgamesh the name of *Utnapishtim* is said to mean "he found life," while in Sumerian his name was *Ziusudra* containing the epithet "the far-distant." This name was rendered as *Xisuthros* by Berossos.

According to the legend the gods grew tired of having to toil for a living, so they created mankind in order to serve the gods. However, they had yet to create a pre-determined lifespan for humans, who lived for centuries and continued to reproduce at such a rate that the earth was soon overcrowded. Unable to sleep because of the constant noise made by humanity, the gods sent a Great Flood in order to reduce human overpopulation. On the advice of Ea, the wise Utnapishtim built an ark for himself, his family, and all the animals. Much of humanity was destroyed but Utnapishtim and those aboard the ark were saved. After seven days when the flood waters had receded and the ship was grounded, Utnapishtim made an offering to the gods. This pleased the gods and consequently saved humanity from total destruction. The gods then gave human beings a fixed life-span and made them mortal, so that they would never again swallow the earth through overpopulation. Later when the Flood story is told to Gilgamesh, Utnapishtim describes how the gods made him immortal—he and his wife were the only humans to be granted eternal life. They achieved the ultimate success in the quest for eternal life.

The ark of Utnapishtim is shown at the top of the card, afloat on the vast expanse of the sea, the surface of which is broken into crystalline patterns of blue and green. Ten fluted cups are shown in a balanced arrangement. At the bottom of the card is a lion-fish and a merman—a creature known as a *kulullu* or "fish-man." This is another hybrid creature whose image, like that of the fish-garbed figure, was considered magically protective. The merman appears to have been one of Ea's creatures. To the right of the top central cup is the cuneiform numeral ten.

Meaning: Complete good fortune, lasting success, pleasure, harmony, security, true happiness that is inspired from above. Satisfaction in one's achievements. True friendship. Domestic happiness. Perfect love. (*Reversed*) A good life that is unappreciated. Sorrow, strife, anger, deceit. Loss of friendship. Disruption.

The Kerub of Cups:
Eagle-headed Spirit

Like the fish-garbed figure, the eagle-headed spirit was often
thought of as one of the Seven Sages (*apkallu*) who lived "in
the first days" before the Great Flood. Statues of this creature were buried in the foundations of homes for protection
from malicious entities and disease. This spirit, depicted in
many examples of Babylonian art, usually carries a *mullilu*
cone and a *banduddu* bucket—ritual symbols used for a cere-
monial purification or a fertility rite sometimes referred to as
the "cone-smearing" ritual, involving the Babylonian Tree of
Life and the divine rite of kingship. The bucket was made of
either metal or wicker. It held holy water or pollen, or perhaps a mixture of both. Pairs of eagle-headed spirits, acting
as gatekeepers and divine guardians of the king, are shown
in relief sculptures that flanked the doorways of palaces.

The authors of the Hebrew scriptures referred to this
figure as the god Nisroch said to have been worshiped by King
Sennacherib. However, there was no Assyro-Babylonian deity
by this name—Nisroch is probably just a corrupt version of
the name of Ninurta (see the King of Disks). It has been suggested by some that the name Nisroch is connected with the
Hebrew word *nesher* or "eagle."

This card shows the eagle-headed spirit with the pine
cone and bucket of holy water, standing ready to purify anyone who enters sacred space.

Meaning: Love of the Divine. Spiritual love and purity. Religious devotion. High ethical standards. Fertility, purification, cleansing, longevity. Divine influence coming through the subconscious mind. (*Reversed*) Loss of faith. Infertility. Impurity, contamination. Unethical. Repressed psychic material spilling over into the conscious mind. Neurosis.

The King of Cups: Apsu

This card shows one of the most ancient of Babylonian deities, the god *Apsu* (Sumerian *Abzu*). According to the Babylonian Epic of Creation, *Enuma Elish*, Apsu was the name of the "first one," the primal masculine deity that existed before heaven and earth existed. He was a gigantic liquid mass as well as a subterranean realm—the "Waters of the Deep"—the fresh "sweet-water" ocean. Apsu was the primeval, underground source of all lakes, rivers, and streams. With his mate Tiamat, who personified the primeval salt-water sea, Apsu sired the first generation of gods.

At a later point in the Creation epic, Apsu cannot sleep because of the noise made by the younger gods, and wishes to destroy them. However, Apsu's plans are foiled by the wise god Ea, "who understands everything." Ea cast a spell over Apsu and killed him in his sleep. He made Apsu's body into his own dwelling place and placed a shrine over it. From that point on, Ea becomes known as the "Lord of the Apsu," the cosmic waters of the Deep.

In the Babylonian world, the earth was believed to be a disk-shaped piece of land that floated above the deep waters of the Apsu. The Babylonian Underworld was situated far below the Apsu, and in some traditions one had to cross a river in order to reach it. The river, called the Hubar, may have been identified with the waters of the Apsu.

The card shows the figure of the ancient god Apsu whose body is composed of the primeval waters, swirling in blue ripples. Below him is a fluted cup.

Meaning: Creative energy which is held in reserve. Creativity channeled into working behind the scenes. A mature man (or person) who is concerned with social responsibility and compassion for the emotions of others—more than his own welfare. A caring husband. Father figure. He is noble, gallant, cultured, creative, sensitive, intelligent, and reserved. A patron of the arts. (*Reversed*) One who suppresses their emotions. A calm exterior masks violent interior. A person who is dishonest, corrupt, domineering and selfish. Scandal.

The Queen of Cups: Nammu

Ancient fragments of theogony lists that existed before the famous Epic of Creation was written suggest that a solitary divine entity, watery in essence, existed before all else, even before the successive lists of divine couples who generated the first gods. This divine being was the goddess *Nammu* "the Lady of the Gods, the Mother who gave birth to the Universe." She was also called "Mother, First One," and the mother who gave birth to heaven and earth," "Mother of everything." In one theogony list, Nammu is placed beyond the ancestors of Anu—even earlier than the most ancient gods. Nammu is the creatrix, the primal matter of the universe, the cosmic primordial sea that existed before all else, and the fertile waters of life. It is possible that the Sumerians conceived of her as having existed eternally.

Nammu is a creator deity and goddess of birth. She is associated with the watery deep and has the power to produce water, especially fresh water. A consort of Anu, this primeval goddess was the mother of Ea and Ereshkigal. In another tradition, she is the mother of Anu and Ki, the archetypal divinities of heaven and earth, as well as other gods. Attended by seven minor goddesses, Nammu is described as the mother of all mortal life and is credited with creating humanity from molded clay. The qualities and attributes of Nammu were later merged into the goddess Aruru.

This card shows the goddess Nammu in her watery realm. She wears a golden diadem topped with rosettes. Before her is a large fluted cup.

Meaning: Reflective force, which mirrors the surrounding energy. A mature woman (or person) of deep emotions, profound sensitivity, and compassion for others. A good mother figure—one who nourishes. She is family-oriented, loving, romantic, kind, patient, wise, honest, virtuous, and highly intuitive. (*Reversed*) Someone who is deceptive, dishonest, unstable, and ungrounded. A dreamer. Unpredictable and unreliable. Perverse and immoral.

The Prince of Cups: Enbilulu

This card shows the god *Enbilulu*, son of the water god Ea. In the Sumerian poem *Enki and the World Order*, the god of wisdom places Enbilulu in charge of streams and rivers. Enbilulu, was called "knower of rivers" and was responsible for maintaining the flow of the sacred rivers Tigris and Euphrates. He was also a divine inspector of canals and irrigation.

Here Enbilulu is shown standing in a river of clear swirling water. A large fluted cup is shown at the right.

Meaning: A force that is volatile, changeable, and mysterious. Erratic energy that can be both sublime and destructive. A fierce nature with a calm exterior. A brother, son, friend, or lover. A messenger with news. A young man (or person) who is intelligent, romantic, artistic, subtle, reserved, and intense. Someone who is complex and conflicted. Passive, withdrawn, and non-committed. (*Reversed*) Narcissistic. A libertine. A heartbreaker. A liar and swindler.

The Princess of Cups: Ishara

The card depicts *Ishara*, a goddess of marriage and child-birth. Like Ishtar she was a goddess of both love and war. In one tradition she was identified as the wife of Dagan, the god of grain. In one prayer which asks the goddess for the removal of sins and deliverance from evil sorceries, Ishara is addressed as the "merciful goddess who heareth supplication." She is also the mother of the *Sebittu* or the "Seven" beneficent gods associated with the star cluster known as the Pleiades in the constellation of Taurus.[5]

Ishara was also concerned with the enforcement of oaths and with divination. One of her earliest symbols was the snake, but in later times she was associated with the scorpion. In astrology she was identified with the constellation known to the Babylonians as the Scorpion (Scorpio).

Here the goddess Ishara is shown holding a *hegallu* vase, ready to pour the water of life. She is the essence of the water itself—as shown by the large face in the water that surrounds her. The face also contains a large "omega" symbol which may have been used to represent the womb. A scorpion is seen at the bottom of the card.

Meaning: Creative, fertile energy that has the power to take on substance or form. Unceasing power to generate new images and ideas. A sister, daughter, friend, or lover. News or a message. A new birth. A young woman (or person) who is gentle, kind, thoughtful, imaginative, artistic, and very gifted. Given to quiet reflection and meditation. (*Reversed*) Someone who is lazy, selfish, and extravagant. Deceptive. Overly dramatic.

1. Budge, E. A. Wallis, *The Babylonian Story of the Deluge and the Epic of Gilgamesh*, 52. (Budge is quoting from R. C. Thompson's *The Epic of Gilgamesh*).

2. Lambert, *Babylonian Wisdom Literature*, 102.

3. Wolkstein, Diane and Samuel Noah Kramer, *Inanna: Queen of Heaven and Earth*, 39.

4. Berossos was a Chaldean Priest of Bel in Babylon [c. 290 B.C.E.] whose books, written in Greek, passed the knowledge of the Babylonians on to the Greek-speaking world.

5. The "Seven" gods were often invoked in magical incantations to combat evil spirits. These are not to be confused with the "Seven" demons who acted as Erra's assistants.

— The Arrows —

The Ace of Arrows: Invocation

The arrow represented in this card is based upon a design seen numerous times in Mesopotamian art. The symbol of the arrow was used on *kudurras* (large polished, inscribed stones) as a symbol of the star Sirius, which was known in Sumerian and Akkadian as "the Arrow." Behind the upright arrow is a bow, indicating that the arrow is about to be fired. At the bottom left of the card is a single cuneiform wedge, indicating the number one.

One form of the arrow was the *marru* or spade, represented by a simple shaft with a triangular head. It was a symbol of the god Marduk. In later Assyrian representations, the marru was transformed into a spear.

Meaning: Great power for good or evil. Triumph of force and will. Tremendous power. Prosperity and fertility. Birth of something new. Always represents invoked force rather than natural force. (*Reversed*) A triumph, but with disastrous results. Tyranny. Friction and conflicts.

The Two of Arrows: Peace Restored

This card shows a peace treaty being struck between two rulers. When one Mesopotamian monarch conquered another, the winner sometimes left the beaten ruler on his throne as a feudal tenant, his status clarified by a vassal-treaty. Monarchs who proved their strength to one another sometimes defined their equal status with a parity treaty. Such treaties, important to ancient diplomacy, were often recorded in writing and witnessed by an official oath-taking ceremony. Blessings were bestowed upon those who abided by the treaty, and curses were heaped upon those who broke them. Breaching a treaty could result in an attack by the aggrieved party.

Many cards in the suit of Arrows are difficult. The balance of the two arrows here, however, has resulted in a card of harmony and peace. In addition, all upward-pointing arrows are a positive sign. With the changeability of the Moon, however, tensions remain and the peace may be fragile. Two kings are shown shaking hands, yet their accompanying soldiers remain armed and ready to go to war again if the treaty is broken. Also seen are two cuneiform wedges, representing the number two.

Meaning: Friendship, union. Balance. Equilibrium. An alliance based on mutual benefit. Quarrels resolved, yet tensions remain. Stalemate, truce, settlement of differences. Friendship in adversity. Uncertain balance. (*Reversed*) Unresolved conflict. Repressed emotions. Deceit on the part of an ally. Breaking of a truce. Lies and treachery.

The Three of Arrows: Sorrow

Once agriculture and animal husbandry began to replace hunting as the primary means of gathering food, the Babylonians engaged in hunting as a means to kill animals that preyed on livestock. Lion hunting in particular became a popular sport among nobles, who hunted the big cats to demonstrate their own courage and skill. Lion hunting was the subject of numerous scenes in Babylonian art.

In this card we see a hapless lioness that has been struck by three arrows. Three large arrows are crossed above the lioness. Unlike the arrows in the previous cards, these arrows point downward, an unfavorable sign. On the right is shown the cuneiform numeral three.

Meaning: Unhappiness, tears, heartbreak, upheaval, disruption, interruption, separation, quarreling. Ending of love. Acceptance of one's pain. (*Reversed*) War, discord, and strife. Great disorder and confusion. Healing process is blocked by the refusal to accept one's pain. Wallowing in misery.

The Four of Arrows: Rest

Mesopotamian rulers often engaged in large-scale engineering projects that created stunning gardens and natural-looking parks both within and outside city walls. Trees and bushes were planted, artificial hills were constructed, and streams were diverted to create lush landscapes. Stocked with exotic animals, these gardens provided shade, beauty, fragrance, and privacy. Royal courtships often took place in such areas.

The lioness from the previous card is now at rest in a garden, her wounds healed. She is shown sleeping under a tree entwined with grapevines. Above the garden, four arrows point upward. At the top of the card is the cuneiform numeral four.

Meaning: Rest from sorrow. Peace after war. Peace through strength. Change for the better. Relaxation of anxiety. Recuperation. Hospitalization. Convalescence, recovery from sickness. A necessary retreat from the world. A needed vacation. Solitude and quiet. (*Reversed*) The vacation is over. Minor misfortunes, disrupted plans. Temporary illness.

The Five of Arrows: Defeat

The *Anzu* (Sumerian *Imdugud*) was a gigantic birdlike monster with the head of a lion. This creature may have been similar in type to the lion-dragon or lion-griffin. The Anzu's beak was said to be like a saw and its hide was as strong as eleven coats of chain mail. When it flapped its wings it caused whirlwinds and sandstorms. In the story of *Gilgamesh, Enkidu, and the Underworld,* this powerful creature built its nest in Inanna-Ishtar's sacred *huluppu* tree until it was chased away by Gilgamesh. In the *Epic of Anzu* the lion-bird steals the Tablet of Destiny from Ellil. The Tablet is a source of great power, for anyone who possesses it can change destiny just by speaking it—anything the owner of the Tablet puts into words becomes reality.

The Anzu's selfish act of theft threatens the very stability of civilization. The gods are fearful, for now Anzu has only to give a spoken command and whoever he curses turns to clay. The warrior god Ninurta is chosen to go after Anzu and retrieve the precious Tablet. When the two combatants meet on the battlefield, Ninurta fires a volley of arrows at the creature. However, Anzu uses the power of the Tablet to make the arrows completely miss their intended target, causing the arrows to turn back into the raw materials they were made from. Disheartened, Ninurta retreats and seeks the council of Ea. Eventually, Ninurta kills the Anzu and returns the Tablet of Destiny to its rightful owner.

The Five of Swords shows the Anzu bird at the moment when he caused Ninurta's arrows to shoot wildly and miss their mark. At this point, Anzu has the upper hand and Ninurta's attempt to subdue him is defeated. Below the creature is the number five written in cuneiform.

Meaning: Conflict, frustration, failure, defeat. Discouragement. The battle is lost. Humiliation. Dishonor. Pride must be swallowed here. (*Reversed*) Despair and defeatism. Pessimism. Weakness. Disaster. Malice. Watch for hidden dangers.

The Six of Arrows: Relief

The goddess *Gula*, the "Great One," was often invoked to cure illness. She was the daughter of the sky god Anu and the earth goddess Urash. Gula was the goddess of healing, the patron goddess of doctors, and she who "understands disease." She was also a midwife to pregnant women. Her Sumerian name was *Ninisina* ("Lady of Isin"), and she was also known by the names *Nintinuga, Ninkarrak,* and *Meme.* Her titles include "Great Healer of the Land" and "Bride of the Earth." Gula was able to heal illness by uttering the appropriate spells and incantations, a method of treatment followed by ancient physicians.

Considered the wife of the god Ninurta, Gula was the mother of two additional gods who were associated with healing: Damu and Ninazu. It is thought that her association with agricultural deities such as Ninurta and Ninazu emphasized her knowledge of the medicinal use of plants. Her role was that of "life-giver" who preserved the health of humans and removed sickness with the merest touch of her hand.

Gula's sacred animal was the dog—an animal which has long been thought to be able to cure disease by licking wounds. Ceramic images of dogs dedicated to Gula were left at her shrines by those who had recovered from illness.

Here we see the goddess Gula standing over the bed of a man who has been shot with an arrow. In one hand the goddess holds a piece of the arrow that she has just removed from the injured man, while in the other hand she holds a healing herb. Gula's faithful dog stands by the bed. Six upright arrows are shown at the top of the card. Above the goddess is the cuneiform numeral six.

Meaning: Success after difficulties and trouble. Reprieve. The danger has passed. A change for the better. A major obstacle has been removed. Earned success. Aid from a helpful person. Journey by water. A spiritual passage. (*Reversed*) More obstacles ahead. Storms are brewing. A bad situation that was quiet is now being stirred up. Strength and vigilance is still needed. Running away from problems will not work.

The Seven of Arrows: Stealth

Closely linked by geography and culture to Mesopotamia, the kingdom of Elam lay to the east of the Land Between the Rivers. The Elamites were dominated by the Akkadian dynasty but eventually regained their independence and invaded Mesopotamia in the thirteenth century B.C.E. The high point of the Elamite conquest ended when King Nebuchadrezzar of Babylon captured the Elamite city of Susa. Later Elam was invaded again by the Assyrian king Ashurbanipal.

This card shows two Elamite soldiers hiding in a field of reeds. Faced with a superior opposing force, they may be hiding in the reeds to escape, or planning an ambush as their only means of attack. In either case, stealth is required. Above and below them are seven arrows which point in both directions. Two of the arrows are haphazardly crossed. Also shown is the cuneiform numeral seven.

Meaning: Unstable effort. Only partial or limited success. Yielding when total victory is within grasp, as if the last reserves of strength were used up. Uncertainty. Direct confrontation is not advised. Stealth and cunning are required. A daring or impulsive act. A Hail-Mary Pass. (*Reversed*) Seek help or advice from others. Learn to listen. Therapy or group support. May indicate overdependence on others. Vacillating and unreliable.

The Eight of Arrows: Restriction

According to the story of *Atrahasis* the Babylonians believed that the gods created humanity to do their work for them. Thus it was only natural for humans to humbly submit to the will and authority of the gods, whom they were obliged to serve.

Human society in the ancient world was ordered along similar lines. When early civilizations expended their territory, losers in battle became the slaves of their conquerors and were used for manual labor. Sometimes, when facing starvation or crushing debt, a poor person in the ancient world would chose slavery—selling himself or a family member—as a means of economic relief.

This card shows a Babylonian laborer carrying a large boulder on his back. He is almost bent over as he struggles to haul the boulder up a hill. His movement is restricted due to the great burden he carries.

Arrows randomly pointing in all directions surround the figure, boxing him in. Beside the figure is the cuneiform numeral eight.

Meaning: Confinement, entrapment, bondage, prison. Enforced isolation. Unexpected difficulties. Limitations caused by one's own lack of awareness. A prison of one's own making. Waste of energy in trivial detail. Hard work for little reward. (*Reversed*) The throwing off of a blindfold. Growing awareness that liberates. Freedom and independence. Release from bondage. Reward for one's efforts.

The Nine of Arrows: Cruelty

As previously indicated, lion hunting was a favorite sport of Babylonian kings. The royal hunt became a standard motif in Neo-Assyrian art. Kings were often depicted hunting lions from chariots, killing them at close range with arrows, spears, or swords. Inscriptions attached to these scenes sometimes described the terror of tributary kings who were forced to take part in the hunt. This was also a spectator sport—onlookers would eat a picnic meal from the safety of a mound or hilltop while the hunt was conducted in a large open field.

Here we see a lion wounded in such a hunt. Enraged, the lion bites furiously at the wheel of the chariot that has attacked him. Nine arrows are shown at the top of the card. Eight of the arrows point downward while the central one points up, symbolizing the courage of the lion as it struggles against cruel odds. Above the wheel of the chariot is the cuneiform numeral nine.

Meaning: Mental cruelty. Despair, distress, loss of a loved one, suffering, illness, burden, oppression. Martyrdom. Overwhelmed and paralyzed with fear. Suffering that may bring new-found strength needed to weather the storm. (*Reversed*) Anger and depression turned inward. Self-hate. Self-blame. Nightmares. Malice, slander.

The Ten of Arrows: Ruin

This card depicts the twin gods *Lugal-irra* ("mighty lord") and *Meslamta-ea* ("he who comes forth from the temple"). These deities, who were sometimes identified with the war god Nergal-Erra, are shown as identical figures—both wear the horned crown of divinity and carry an axe and a mace. They were considered guardians of the gates of the underworld, whose duty was to dismember the dead as they entered the Land of No Return.

Superlatively skilled in guarding doorways, effigies of the "Great Twins" were often buried at entrances to buildings. Astrologically, Lugal-irra and Meslamta-ea are attributed to the constellation of Gemini.

Here we see the Great Twins standing before the darkened opening to the underworld. Ten arrows, all pointing downward, are falling to the earth. At the lower right is the cuneiform numeral ten.

Meaning: Ruin, misfortune, affliction, defeat, disruption, failure. Hitting rock bottom. (*Reversed*) The worst has already happened—things can only get better from here. Temporary gain that will not be permanent. Real change is needed to make things better.

The Kerub of Arrows:
Human-headed Spirit

The human-headed spirit is another protective kerub or genie often portrayed in Babylonian art. The Sumerian term for this type of beneficent, protective male spirit may have been *Alad* (*Sedu* in Akkadian). Female spirits were known as *Lama* (*Lamassu* in Akkadian).

As was the case with the eagle-headed spirit, this kerub was considered one of the antediluvian Sages.

In this card the kerub is a winged male spirit who holds a flowing branch in one hand and a sacrificial deer in the other. To the right of the figure is an upright arrow.

Meaning: Divine Wisdom and understanding. Spiritual awareness coming through the conscious mind. Intellectual aid, intelligence gained. Knowledge is increased. Gain and increase through reasoned response. (*Reversed*) Divine wisdom is not forthcoming. Lack of awareness. Information that doesn't help the situation.

The King of Arrows: Ellil

Head of the younger generation of gods *Ellil,* son of Anu and Ki, was the lord of wind and storm. In authority he was second only to his father Anu. His Sumerian name was *Enlil,* and after 2500 B.C.E. he was effectively the national god of Sumer. His name means "lord wind" and he was said to have separated his parents (heaven and earth) with a pickaxe. While Anu was king of heaven, Ellil was king of the earth. Considered "king of all the lands," the other gods were not even allowed to look upon his splendor and yet they were eager for his blessing. His other titles were "raging storm," "great mountain," "wild bull," "father of the gods," "establisher of kingship," and "the king of heaven and earth." Like Anu, he had a reserved promenade in the heavens, but his usual abode was the Great Mountain of the East.

Ellil symbolized the forces of nature and was considered to be the master of humanity's fate—he ruled over disasters, prosperity, abundance, and destiny. It was Ellil who kept the Tablet of Destiny which contained the fates of both gods and humans. He watched over the welfare of the people of Sumer and bestowed kingship upon Sumerian rulers. Later myths and poems portray him as a beneficent creator god who produced the most fruitful aspects of the universe: he brought forth the dawn at the beginning of day, he created seeds, plants, trees, and the fruits of harvest. He is also credited with inventing the pickaxe and the plough. It was Ellil who established the productivity of the land and made agriculture possible.

Lord Wind also has the power to confer kingship and even "god-ship" (*ellilu'tu* or "Ellilship")—he could promote other deities to new and higher positions of authority. In addition "the word of Ellil" is a form of pure unspoken wisdom— the god's will-in-action—that causes creation and change, not unlike the Hermetic idea of the Logos.

Ellil was a friend to humanity. However, like the Hebrew god Yahweh, his anger could be aroused by human wickedness. It was Ellil who advocated that the gods unleash the Great Flood upon humanity in the story of *Atrahasis*. The unpleasant task of enforcing human calamities decreed by the assembly of gods fell upon Ellil. Because of this, he has usually been accused of being a severe and destructive deity by later scholars. By contrast, Sumerian hymns venerate him as a gracious father figure who protects his people:

> *Enlil, whose command is far-reaching, whose word is holy,*
> *The lord whose pronouncement is unchangeable,*
> *who forever decrees destinies,*
> *Whose lifted eye scans the lands,*
> *Whose lifted beam searches the heart of all the lands,*
> *Enlil who sits broadly on the white dais,*
> *Who perfects the decrees of power, lordship, and princeship,*
> *[. . .]*
> *The arrogant, the agreement-violator,*
> *He does not tolerate their evil in the city. [. . .]*
>
> *The earth gods bow down in fear before him,*
> *The heaven-gods humble themselves before him [. . .]*
> *Nippur—the shrine where dwells the father, [. . .]*

Its prince "great mountain," Father Enlil,
Has established its seat on the dais of the Ekur, lofty shrine;
The temple–its decrees like heaven cannot be overturned,
Its pure rites like the earth cannot be shattered, [. . .]
Its words are prayers,
Its utterances are supplication . . .,
Its ritual is precious,
Its feast flow with fat and milk, are rich with abundance,
Its storehouses bring happiness and rejoicing,
Enlil's house, it is a mountain of plenty . . .[1]

Ellil's wife was the goddess Ninlil (also called *Sud* and *Mulliltu*). The couple's divine children included Shamash, Sin, Adad, Ishtar, and Nusku.

Here we see the great god Ellil in the midst of storm clouds, holding an arrow.

Meaning: Violent, fiery energy that is unstable and extremely volatile. Swift and agitated energy that is unpredictable. A mature man (or person) of power and authority. He is intelligent, aggressive, rational, and obstinate. Someone who believes strongly in justice and the law. (*Reversed*) Someone who sits in judgment of others and looks out for his own interests. He may be cruel, insensitive, unjust, and sadistic. He is tyrannical, crafty, domineering, and deceitful.

The Queen of Arrows:
Ishtar of Arba'il

The great goddess Ishtar had many different aspects to her personality, the result of a number of different and originally independent local goddesses being merged into one deity. She continued to be venerated under many local manifestations. In Assyria Ishtar of Arba'il (or Arbela) was especially renowned for being a goddess of war. However, the goddess rarely engaged in bloody combat herself. Instead, she operated more as a war strategist whose forceful authority commanded obedience and respect.

Fond of battle, Ishtar would stand beside her favorite kings as they fought. It was believed that the bond between the goddess and the king was a conjugal one: if she loved the ruler and considered him a "spouse," she would bestow her blessings upon him and grant him kingship, conquest, and victory in warfare. On the other hand, if the king fell out of Ishtar's favor—or if the goddess no longer found him attractive or desired him as a mate—he would be defeated. Being "married" to Ishtar meant that the king moved in the social circle of the gods. Their divinity and power were thereby extended to him.

In her warrior aspect, Ishtar is often depicted as a winged goddess who is armed to the teeth, grasping her double-lion-headed scepter, with a case of arrows slung over her shoulder. Her commands were not to be opposed.

If the Babylonians regarded her [. . .] as the great mother-goddess, the Assyrians took but little notice of this side of her character. To them she was a veritable Valkyrie, and as the Assyrians grew more and more military so she became the war-goddess and less the nature-mother [. . .] She appeared in dreams to the war-loving Kings of Assyria, encouraging and heartening them with words of cheer to further military exploits. Fire was her raiment, and as became a goddess of battle, her appearance was terrific. [. . .] she is at times brought into close association with Asshur she is never regarded as his wife. She is not the consort of any god, but an independent goddess in her own right, standing alone, equal with Asshur and dependent of no other deity.[2]

In an oracle addressed to King Esarhaddon, Ishtar reassures the king of her support:

Esarhaddon, king of the lands, fear not!
What wind has risen against you,
whose wing I have not broken?
Your enemies will roll before you like ripe apples.
I am the Great Lady, I am Ishtar of Arbela
Who cast your enemies before your feet.
What words have I spoken to you that you could not rely upon?
I am Ishtar of Arbela.
I will flay your enemies and give them to you.
I am Ishtar of Arbela. I will go before you and behind you.
Fear not! You are paralyzed,
but in the midst of woe I will rise up and sit down beside you
By the mouth of Ishtar [. . .] of Arbela.[3]

Here we see Ishtar of Arba'il, stern and red-eyed, wearing the horned crown of divinity topped by the head of a lion, her sacred animal. There is a large arrow to her left.

Meaning: Creative, enduring, and resilient energy. A mature woman (or person) who is intensely perceptive, observant, alert, intelligent, quick-witted, decisive, authoritative, confident, and self-reliant. (*Reversed*) She may be selfish, malicious, domineering, cruel, ruthless, deceitful, and spiteful. A dangerous enemy. A widow. Mourning and sorrow.

The Prince of Arrows: Erra

Erra, the son of Ellil (or Anu), was a god of hunting, warfare, pestilence, and the scorching heat of the sun. He is also known as *Nergal* and as *Engidudu*, the "lord who prowls by night." His other name of *Erragal* or *Erakal* ("Erra the Great") was possibly just the phonetic pronunciation of Nergal, and was probably the origin for the Greek Herakles. Originally separate gods, Erra and Nergal later become merged into one deity and lost their individual characteristics.

As Nergal, he was considered the husband of Ereshkigal and a god of the underworld. According to the story of *Nergal and Ereshkigal*, the gods held a great banquet. Because Ereshkigal could not leave the underworld, she was invited to send her messenger, Namtar, to receive her portion. When Namtar arrived, all the gods stood up as a sign of respect to his mistress—all except for Nergal, who was promptly ordered to go down to the underworld to be punished for his insolence by the Queen of Death. Ea advised him not to eat or drink anything in the underworld, and not to succumb to the temptations of Ereshkigal. However, the seductive charms of the dark goddess overtook him, and he lay with her for six days. On the seventh day, the goddess let him return for a while to the upper world, but she soon longed for his touch. She threatened to end all fertility and life on earth unless Nergal was returned to her. Upon his return Nergal grabbed Ereshkigal by the hair and pulled her off her throne in a passionate embrace. After another six days of intimacy, the couple is married and Nergal is made King of the underworld.

As a symbol of the destructive power of the sun, Nergal-Erra's journey into the underworld represents the sun's passage through the Land of Death at night, and it brings to mind the Greek legend of Persephone and Hades.

In astrology Erra is attributed to the planet Mars. He commands the *Sebittu* or seven demons who rally to his side in warfare.[4] Erra's name was often invoked in prayers designed to prevent the hazards that were identified with him. One prayer to the god describes him as:

> *The mighty, the valiant, the lord of power!*
> *Who giveth the victory, who establisheth strength!*
> *King of the battle, the wise, the courageous, the invincible!*[5]

Erra is sometimes called "the Lord of Justice," "the Lord of Limits," and "God of Necessity." He is seen as a harsh but indispensable force. His virtues are those of the warrior and the solider—strength, fearlessness, and steely determination. He does not hesitate to mete out harsh punishment in compliance with the requirements of justice.

Erra is usually depicted as a man dressed in a long robe, stepping forward with one leg barred. He often carries a scimitar and sometimes holds the double lion-headed scepter. Here we see the god Erra armed with scimitar, bow and arrows. He is posed to fire an arrow in battle.

Meaning: Intellectual force that destroys ideas as quickly as they are created. A harsh force that is too volatile to be enduring. A young man (or person) who is full of ideas, thoughts, and designs. He tends to start things and never finish them. He is brave, skillful, and strong, yet emotionally detached. The archetypal warrior. (*Reversed*) Someone who is reckless, irresponsible, impatient, and out of control. He may be a fanatic. He may be tactless, intolerant, harsh, malicious, and treacherous. A false friend.

The Princess of Arrows: Ninlil

The goddess *Ninlil* (also known as *Mullissu, Mulliltu,* and *Sud*) was the wife of the air god Ellil. Her name of Ninlil means "lady wind." Known for her benevolent nature, Ninlil often intervened on behalf of humans when her husband was angry with them. In addition to her role as an air goddess, she was also a goddess of grain. Ninlil was the daughter of Haia, the god of stores and Ninsebargunna, the goddess of barley.

In the story of *Enlil and Ninlil,* the storm god Enlil (Ellil) sees the beautiful virgin goddess Ninlil bathing in a stream and rapes her. The young goddess goes before the assembly of gods to demand justice. Scandalized by the whole affair, the gods decide that Ellil is to be banished to the underworld for his offence. Ninlil, pregnant with their son Nanna (Sin, the moon god) and with new-found feelings toward her lover, follows him into exile. This troubles Ellil who worries that his son might be born in the underworld and forced to dwell there rather than rule the night sky as the moon should. To prevent this from happening, he disguises himself by taking on the forms of three underworld guards. Incognito, he impregnates Ninlil three more times. The resulting offspring are three underworld gods (including Nergal and Ninazu in some traditions) who are able to take Sin's place in the netherworld. As a result the moon god is free to rise up to heaven.

It has been suggested by some that Ellil's three acts of tender courtship while in disguise was designed to make up for his earlier violation of Ninlil. The goddess's loyalty to Ellil makes her a most revered wife—sharing in his divine title and authority.

Ninlil's other divine children included Shamash, Adad, Ishtar, and Nusku. Ninlil's name appears as the most loved of mothers in hymns dedicated to her sons. Some Babylonian prayers were addressed to Ninlil in an attempt to gain her favor and the influence she had on her powerful spouse.

In Assyria, Ninlil became the spouse of Ashur, the primary god of the empire. In ancient Greece she was known as *Mylitta*, a variant of her Akkadian name of *Mulliltu* which meant "the one who brings to birth." The lion was her sacred animal.

Here we see the wind goddess Ninlil standing on clouds. She holds an arrow in one hand and a bow in the other. Unlike the warrior Erra of the previous card, the gentle goddess is not preparing to fire the arrow.

Meaning: Decisive, stabilizing force in an erratic environment. A young woman (or person) who is assertive, self-confident, observant, emotionally detached, distant. She shows intensity and dexterity. A skilled negotiator, debater, or emissary. (*Reversed*) She is unsympathetic, insensitive, wrathful, vindictive, cunning, devious, and frivolous. A pretender. Prone to spying, rumor-mongering, and meddling into the affairs of others. Bad news.

1. Kramer, Samuel, *The Sumerians: Their History, Culture, and Character,* 120.

2. Spence, Lewis, *Myths and Legends of Babylonia & Assyria,* 213–214.

3. Bottéro, Jean, *Religion in Ancient Mesopotamia,* 173–174.

4. These "Seven" demons are not to be confused with the "Seven" beneficent gods of the Pleiades.

5. King, Leonard W., *Babylonian Magic and Sorcery,* 110–111.

— The Disks —

The Ace of Disks: Materiality

The disk represented in this card is based on the star-disk, an emblem which permeates Babylonian art. The eight-pointed star probably originated as a general symbol of astral significance. It was later used to indicate the planet Venus and was a symbol of the goddess Ishtar.

The Mesopotamina emblems of the star-disk and the sun-disk look very similar. However, the eight rays of the star-disk are straight, while in the sun-disk four of the eight rays are wavy.

The cuneiform script at the bottom of the card indicates a Babylonian word *kimu* meaning "grain." At the top of the card is a single cuneiform wedge, the Babylonian number one.

Meaning: Materiality in all senses, good and evil. Material gain, prosperity, labor, power, wealth. Attainment. A new enterprise. Security, firm foundation. Faculty of sensation. (*Reversed*) Corruption caused by money. Greed, avarice. Miserly. Abuse of power. Clinging to old and familiar routines.

The Two of Disks: Change

This card shows two large disks one above the other, ornamented with Mesopotamian decorative patterns. At the bottom of the card are two primitive "eye idols." These are extremely simplified versions of the same votive statutues that are shown in the Four of Wands, and they were employed for the same purpose—they were left in a god's temple to serve as reverent surrogates for their human counterparts. These abstract humanoid figures had a flat body and a long neck surmounted by a large pair of eyes. The eye was considered a potent magical symbol in Mesopotamia.

The two figurines shown in this card are symbols of a hoped-for change in circumstance brought about by the blessings of deity.

Meaning: Pleasant change, alteration of gain and loss, cycles of flux and reflux. Harmony in the midst of change. Juggling and balancing of opposites. Change is imminent. News, communications, or journeys having to do with business. A light-hearted, optimistic outlook on life. (*Reversed*) Pretending that things are OK when they're not. Warnings signs are ignored. Foolhardy. Not taking things seriously results in loss of opportunity.

The Three of Disks: Work

The Babylonians were a hard-working people. Their industrious nature coupled with the fertility of the land meant that surplus food could be produced in the ancient world. This in turn led to more specialization of the labor force, since many people did not have to till the land or raise their own livestock. Individuals with the skills to produce other goods and commodities could barter their services for food. A wide assortment of occupations soon developed: potters, weavers, metal smiths, millers, teachers, scribes, merchants, doctors, soldiers, priests, bricklayers, canal diggers, and more.

Babylonian women were fully engaged in the raising of children and numerous household tasks that were vital to the welfare of the family.

One Sumerian goddess was especially associated with work of the home and hearth. *Uttu* was the goddess of weaving. She was the daughter of Enki (Ea) and Ninkurra, goddess of mountain pastures. With Enki's seed she gives birth to eight plants, the original seedlings of all vegetation in the paradisiacal land of Dilmun.

In the narrative poem *Enki and the World Order*, the god of wisdom puts various deities in charge of different occupations. Enki put Uttu "the trustworthy woman" in charge of spinning, weaving, the making of clothing and jewelry, and everything "which is woman's task." Her dexterity in weaving earned her the title "Skillful Woman." She is the Sumerian ideal of a good mother and wife.

The symbol of the name *Uttu* was also used to mean "spider." This associated the goddess with the industriousness of the spider, who spins a web to create a home and catch food.

Here we see Uttu as she works, spinning thread. Beside her is a spider, her sacred animal, sitting in a web. At the top of the card are three disks, one which bears the image of a lion-fish, and two which bear the image of the *suhurmasu* or "goat-fish" of Capricorn (alluding to the astrological decan of the card). In the center is the cuneiform numeral three.

Meaning: Business ventures, employment, commercial transactions. Passion for work. Professional craftsmanship. Proficiency in a profession, trade, or skill. Construction, creation, realization, increase in material matters. (*Reversed*) Mediocrity in work, shoddy craftsmanship. Laziness, weakness. No improvement. Work that one enjoys but is not profitable.

The Four of Disks: Security

The most unique structure built in the Mesopotamian world was without a doubt the ziggurat, which comes from the Akkadian word *zigguratu* meaning "peak" or "high place." Sometimes called a "stepped pyramid" the ziggurat was a multilevel brick platform located on a terrace. The four corners of most ziggurats pointed to the four cardinal directions. A shrine was located on the summit and rituals dedicated to the gods took place there. Ziggurats were sometimes referred to in ancient times as "house of the mountain," or "mountain of the storm," indicating that these man-made mountains were created to be the abode of the gods who were thought to live in high mountain peaks. It was believed that the god of the temple would descend from heaven and dwell amongst his people within the high shrine atop the ziggurat.

Mesopotamia's largest ziggurat, located in the city of Babylon, was called *Etemenanki*, or "the link between heaven and earth." The Greek historian Herodotus described the shrine at its summit as the site of a sacred marriage ceremony between the god Marduk and a mortal priestess.

Unlike Egyptian pyramids, which were built in remote deserts and sealed up for the use of the dead, Babylonian ziggurats were located in the center of busy cities and designed for the use of the living. Believing that their patron deity dwelled within their midst must have given the Babylonians a sense of security in an uncertain world.

In this card we see a ziggurat on a hill. Above it are four disks—two which bear the image of the goat-fish (Capricorn) and two that bear the image of the sun-disk. These symbols in the disks allude to the astrological decan of the card. In the center is the cuneiform numeral four.

Meaning: Material stability and security. Holding onto possessions. Protecting what you have. Fortification. Preparing the groundwork. Gain of money or influence, a gift, inheritance, assured material gain, success. Establishment of a commercial empire. Power achieved through acquisition. Business obstacles removed. (*Reversed*) Bloated bureaucracy. Greed. Stagnant and resistant to positive change. Material instability and loss. Business obstacles. Structural breakdown. Lack of security.

The Five of Disks: Trouble

This card describes a scene from the *Epic of Gilgamesh*. After defeating the monster Humbaba, Gilgamesh returns to Uruk, bathes, and dresses in fine garments. The goddess Ishtar is smitten with his physical beauty and offers to take him as a lover. Gilgamesh rejects her advances, however, recalling tales of how cruelly the goddess often treated her lovers. Furious at his refusal, Ishtar implores the god Anu to release the Bull of Heaven to reek havoc upon the city of Uruk and destroy Gilgamesh in the process. Anu is hesitant at first, but when Ishtar threatens to release the dead from the underworld, he does as she asks.

The Bull of Heaven is set loose and manages to kill scores of young men from Uruk until it is slain by Gilgamesh. Ishtar is beside herself with rage at the death of the Bull. Gilgamesh tears the bull apart and throws its hindquarters at the angry goddess. Keeping the bull's horns as a trophy, Gilgamesh and Enkidu celebrate their great victory. Unwittingly, however, their actions incur the wrath of the gods, resulting in Enkidu's death.

In this card we see Gilgamesh tearing apart the Bull of Heaven, attributed to Taurus. Five disks surround the central figures. Above the head of Gilgamesh is the cuneiform numeral five.

Meaning: Material trouble. Loss of profession or position. Setback. Loss. Support is needed. Time to be careful. Spiritual impoverishment. (*Reversed*) Disorder, chaos, ruin. Material loss but spiritual gain. Seek other avenues.

The Six of Disks: Assistance

One type of god in the Babylonian pantheon was the *Lahmu* which meant "hairy one." This term sometimes referred to a single deity, while at other times it was used to describe a pair or group of these deities.

In the story of *Enuma Elish*, the male *Lahmu* and the female *Lahamu* were one of the first primordial couples listed in the theogony, born from the union of Apsu and Tiamat. Some have suggested that Lahmu and Lahamu were represented by the silt of the seabed. In the epic of creation, this couple in turn produced Ansar and Kisar, who were the parents of the sky god Anu.

A beneficent and protective deity, Lahmu was associated with Ea and later with Marduk. Small statutes of Lahmu were buried in the foundations of building to guard against illness and evil demons. Lahmu was usually represented as a bearded figure with long curly hair.

Ea's temple in Eridu was said to contain fifty lahmu who controlled the ocean and the availability of fish for food. They are often shown holding a *hegallu* vase which overflows with water.

At the bottom of the card are two lahmu gods who both hold vases of overflowing water. They are assisting two thirsty buffalo by providing water from the vases. Above them are six disks, three containing the image of the moon-disk, and three containing the image of a bearded bull, alluding to the astrological decan of the card. In the upper part of the scene is the cuneiform numeral six.

Meaning: Success and gain in material undertakings, prosperity in business, gain in power, rank and influence. Problem solved. Hopes fulfilled. Sharing one's good fortune with others through charity, philanthropy, and gifts. Fortunate and generous. Giving what is needed, not what is wanted. (*Reversed*) Miserly. Selfishness. Careless or wasteful with money. Dependent on the charity of others. Debt. Loss through theft. Envy and jealousy. Charity that has an ulterior motive.

The Seven of Disks: Inertia

In ancient Mesopotamia the agricultural year began in late fall or early winter with the sowing of crops. The early spring growing season was an anxious time when farmers had to fend off locusts, hungry rodents, and crop-killing diseases. Depending on the type of crops grown, harvest took place in April and May. Barley, the primary crop, was harvested in late March at the time of the spring equinox. This was considered the beginning of the ancient month of Nisan and the start of the Babylonian New Year.

This card shows the Bull of Heaven, which the Babylonians associated with the constellation of Taurus. In the Sumerian version of *The Descent of Inanna,* the Bull of Heaven is named *Gugalanna,* the husband of Ereshkigal. The reason given by Inanna-Ishtar for entering the underworld is to witness the funeral rites of Gugalanna. The astrological interpretation of "the funeral rites of Gugalanna" is the six-week time period beginning in mid-January that the constellation of Taurus was below the Mesopotamian horizon. The return of Taurus to the Sumerian sky in March was correlated to the agricultural cycle and the annual reappearance of the shepherd god Dumuzi (Tammuz) from the underworld. Dumuzi was often referred to as a bull, and it interesting to note that in different traditions both Dumuzi and Gugalanna were considered to be husbands of Inanna.

Ritual lamentations in honor of Dumuzi-Tammuz began at harvest time, when the cutting of grain represented the death of the shepherd god. The rites of mourning intensified

during mid-summer, when the hot season made the land barren and dried up milk production from sheep and goats.

Here we see the Bull of Heaven resting by the dark mouth
of the underworld, suggesting the bleak period when Tammuz is lost to the land of the living. The bull of Taurus is in-
active—inert. Above the figure of the bull are seven disks
which together form the geomantic figure of Rubeus. In the
center of the card is the cuneiform numeral seven.

Meaning: Small accomplishments but complete success still
lacking. Past successes not followed up. Inaction, delay, hold-
up. Resting on one's laurels when there is still more to do.
Much work for small gains. (*Reversed*) Money worries. Un-
profitable speculation and employment. Bad loans, gambling.

The Eight of Disks: Skill

In their quest to resolve the age-old questions about how the universe functioned, the priests of Mesopotamia looked to the heavens for answers. Acute observations of the celestial bodies lead them to discover that ancient science we term astrology—an art they became quite experienced at.

The Sumerians were keenly aware of the cyclical movements of the constellations, which were tied to the seasons. Temple scribes kept long lists of stars and constellations. The main system of Sumerian astrology was a method of interpreting star-omens. The constellations were named after various deities and each was assigned different qualities.

Gradually the Babylonian star-gazers noticed that there was one area of sky through which the planets and luminaries of the sun and moon traveled, and this belt or circle of sky included nineteen separate constellations that were used to distinguish twelve different segments of the belt. It was also noticed that the lunar cycle was completed twelve times a year. By 600–500 B.C.E., astrologers reduced the number of zodiacal constellations to twelve. Thus the first twelve-sign zodiac was a creation of the Mesopotamians' aptitude for star-gazing.

Ancient astrologers saw the stars as the embodiment of the gods, whose movements in the night sky expressed the divine law which governed the cosmos. The star-gazers could predict the various ways that the movements of heavenly bodies would affect the lives of human beings. The earliest known personal horoscope using the zodiac as a map of the heavens at the time of a person's birth dates to 410 B.C.E.

Here we see two skilled Babylonian priests studying the stars of the night sky and recording their observations on a clay tablet. Above them are eight disks, four containing the image of the rosette and four that are adorned with the sun-disk. Above the priests is the cuneiform numeral eight.

Meaning: Apprenticeship. Craftsmanship. Ambition. Industry. Skilled work that pays off. Talent. Artistry. Satisfaction in one's handiwork. Career training and experience. Developing new skills. Labor brings its rewards. A job well done. Prudence. (*Reversed*) Lack of ambition, unfulfilled ambition. Unsatisfying work. No pride in one's work. Envy, Jealousy. Nitpicking, fussy, and overly critical. May be "penny wise and pound-foolish."

The Nine of Disks: Gain

The epic of creation known as *Enuma Elish* was not the only Babylonian narrative that sought to explain the origin of the universe. Different cities sometimes had their own creation stories that varied substantially from each other. The *Theogeny of Dunnu* featured Plough and Earth as the two primeval forces which initiated creation. According to the story, Plough married Earth and produced Sea, Furrows, and Cattle God. The Cattle God and Sea then sired the Flocks God who married River. From this union was born the Herdsman God and Pasture-and-Poplar, who in turn sired the deities Haharnum and Belet-seri. Each new generation of gods that is created completely replaces (kills) the generation that came before it, suggesting a connection with the agricultural cycle of planting, growth, and harvest. At a certain point in the story beginning with the New Year, the younger generation of gods permits the previous generation to co-exist with it, rather than eliminating it.

In this card we see a plough, representing one of the primary forces of creation. United with the earth, the plough has cut deep furrows into the soil as a prelude to the planting of grain that will provide food for successive generations. The nine disks that are shown in the soil represent the seeds of growth for a future harvest. Five of the disks are ornamented with the rosette, and the remaining four are decorated with the star-disk of Venus. On the upper right of the card is the cuneiform numeral nine.

Meaning: Personal success. Personal accomplishment. Self-reliance. Solitary enjoyments. Much increase of goods, material gain, inheritance, enjoyment of comforts. Plans coming to fruition. Security. Well-being. Good sense, order, and discipline. Appreciation and honors. (*Reversed*) Projects abandoned. Irresponsibility. Loss. Present stability will not last. Arrogance. Prosperity gained through devious, illegal, or immoral means.

The Ten of Disks: Completion

This card shows a stylized tree with a serpent curled around its base and an eagle perched at its summit. It portrays an early scene in the story of *The Epic of Etana* wherein the two creatures have pledged mutual cooperation to each other. At this point in the story, they live in harmony and balance each other at either end of the tree.

The motif of a tree that is the abode of both a bird and a serpent is also found in the Sumerian story of *Gilgamesh and the Huluppu Tree.*

Serpents were often portrayed as magically protective creatures in seal designs and small figurines. The perched bird was used as a symbol of the agricultural-warrior god Ninurta.

In the modern Hermetic tradition, the eagle is emblematic of the human soul, able to soar on wings of spiritual ascent, while the serpent is seen as a creature of wisdom that winds its way upward through the branches of the Tree of Life, gaining valuable experience as it climbs.

In this card, the image of the serpent curled around the base of the tree with the eagle at the top is meant to evoke the symbolism of the Tree of Life as well as the winged caduceus, which is an expression of equilibrium—of opposing forces balancing one another in order to create a higher, more centered whole.

Ten disks all containing the image of the rosette are shown as the fruit of the tree. Beside the eagle is the cuneiform numeral ten.

Meaning: Attainment, realization, accomplishment, culmination. Riches, wealth, gain, completion of material fortune. Security and success shared with family and friends. Family wealth, inheritance. Wills, dowries. Family home. Family business. A time of good harvest. (*Reversed*) Robbery. Theft. Gambling. Uncertainty. Family misfortune, loss of inheritance. Breakup of an estate or legal troubles after a death. Comforts taken for granted.

Kerub of Disks:
Human-headed Bull

The human-headed bull is a very powerful winged guardian spirit whose colossal image was carved into the stone gateways of royal palaces. Usually two such colossi flanked the entryway into a palace. Someone entering the palace gates could not help but be in awe of these huge guardians—their eyes staring forward like watchful sentinels, or with heads turned inward as if to scrutinize the mortal entering therein. These were not really bulls at all but sacred beings, the gods or genii of holy places. The physical make-up of these creatures was meant to convey the intelligence of man (the head) mixed with the swiftness of an eagle (the wings) and the raw physical power of a bull (the body). It is possible that this type of creature, like the bull-man, might have been called *gud-alim* in Sumerian and *kusarikku* in Akkadian—named after the extinct Mesopotamian bison. The Assyrians called these creatures *aladlammu*. The feminine form of this creature was *apsasu*.

Above the human-headed bull in the upper right of the card is a single disk.

Meaning: A guardian appears to offer assistance. Divine aid manifesting in the physical plane. Manifestation of spiritual power. Materialization of what had previously been abstract and theoretical. (*Reversed*) Divine aid does not materialize. Dispersion, diffusion, the breaking down of the material. Scattering of the whole into its various parts.

The King of Disks: Ninurta

The worship of the war god *Ninurta*, "lord of arable earth," was popular in Mesopotamia from the earliest days of ancient Sumer through the later days of Assyria. He is sometimes referred to as *Ninib* by nineteenth-century authors. The Hebrew authors of the Bible referred to Ninurta as *Nimrod,* "the mighty hunter before the Lord."

This god was closely associated with the agricultural god *Ningirsu* ("lord of Girsu"), whom some consider an older, local form of Ninurta. The two deities eventually became merged into one god who was paradoxically associated with battle and agriculture—he was both a farmer and a warrior. Ninurta is "Lord Plough" and "Master of the Fields."

Both of these facets of Ninurta are revealed in the story of *Ninurta and Asag* from the Sumerian poem entitled *Lugale*. The story tells how the god destroys Asag, a monstrous demon of disease.

Asag led a rebellion of plants and stones which rolled down from the mountains to crush the Mesopotamian cities of the plains. The hero defeats Asag by using rain to subdue the monster's dust storm. Afterwards Ninurta raises up the foothills and creates canals for the water's flow. Using the stones that had previously tried to kill him, Ninurta built a huge stone wall in front of Sumer to hold back floods—channeling the water into the Tigris River where the overflow could be used to irrigate crops and facilitate farming.

What had been scattered, he gathered,
What of the Kur had been scattered,

He guided and hurled into the Tigris,
The high waters it pours over the fields.
Behold, now, everything on earth,
Rejoiced afar at Ninurta, the king of the land,
The fields produced abundant grain,
The vineyard and orchard bore their fruit,
The harvest was heaped up in granaries and hills,
The lord made mourning to disappear from the land,
He made happy the spirit of the gods.[1]

The god then examines all the various types of rock and gives each stone a specific function. Those rocks that had switched their loyalty from Asag to Ninurta were rewarded, becoming precious gemstones attributed to the gods.

Ninurta's fame as an agricultural deity was evident in *The Instruction of Ninurta*, the title given to an ancient Sumerian "farmer's almanac" which describes how to grow barley. The almanac called Ninurta "the son and true farmer of Enlil."

There were also many stories extolling the god's conquests in battle, and he became a favorite personal deity of Assyrian kings. Ninurta had a stormy temperament due to his origin as an ancient thunder god of the spring rain. His many titles include "the courageous one" and "mighty one of the gods." In addition to his victory over the demon Asag, the poem *Lugal-e* recounts several of Ninurta's battles and describes how he defeated a lion, a buffalo, a six-headed ram, a seven-headed serpent, and other adversaries. Ninurta's victories were most likely the inspiration for the Greek stories of the Labors of Heracles.

In the *Epic of Anzu*, Ninurta is the champion chosen by the gods to pursue the monstrous Anzu or lion-headed bird who stole the Tablet of Destiny from Ellil. His first attack on Anzu fails, but urged on by Ea, Ninurta tries again and batters the bird with powerful winds, breaking its wings. After killing the Anzu, Ninurta returns the Tablet of Destiny to Ellil.

Ninurta has a powerful weapon called *Sharur* or "smasher of thousands," a mace which had its own intelligence and the power of speech. The warrior-farmer also has the power to control the Seven of Battle, who can create whirlwinds. Ninurta was considered the son of Ellil and either Aruru or Ninlil, although the Assyrians later changed his parents to Ashur and Ishtar. His wife was Gula, the goddess of healing.

In this card, the god Ninurta is shown with his symbol, the plow. He is portrayed as a rugged-looking man who is a skilled farmer and a seasoned warrior. No stranger to work, he is at home in the barley field as well as the battlefield. At the top of the card is a disk.

Meaning: Stimulating and fertilizing energy that causes growth and material production. Expansive force. A mature man (or person) who is laborious, patient, practical, loyal, reliable, brave, resourceful, methodical, deliberate, and conservative. He is a good worker and a sturdy provider. A good businessman. (*Reversed*) He can be greedy, materialistic, dull, slow, unintelligent, or crude. A corrupt businessman or ruthless competitor.

The Queen of Disks: Gestinana

Gestinana, daughter of the sheep goddess Sirtur (or Duttur) was the loyal sister of Dumuzi (Tammuz), shepherd god of vegetation, and the wife of the tree god Ningiszida. Her name comes from the word *geshtin*, which means "grapevine" identifying her as the goddess of viniculture and the "vine of heaven." She was also called *Belili*. She is sometimes equated with the Akkadian goddess *Belet-seri*, "lady of the open country-side."

In the Sumerian story of the *Descent of Inanna*, Gestinana is called the "wise woman who knows the meaning of dreams." Dumuzi calls upon her to interpret a disturbing dream. The goddess realizes that the dream is a sign of her brother's impending demise, and together they flee to Gestinana's home. When galla demons arrive to carry Dumuzi off to the underworld, she refuses to tell them where he is hiding, even under torture. Eventually, the demons find the shepherd god and catch him. A desperate Dumuzi prays to the sun god to change him into a gazelle, so he can escape from the demons. He is caught a second time, however, and the gallas drag him off to the underworld.

Gestinana laments the loss of her brother and thus became known as "she who always weeps." She volunteers to share Dumuzi's fate. Full of remorse, Inanna (Ishtar) takes pity on her, and together they set out for the underworld. When they find Dumuzi weeping, Inanna decrees that Gestinana will take Dumuzi's place in the underworld for half of the year. As a result, Gestinana and Dumuzu share the burden, alternating six-month periods spent in the underworld, resulting in the change of seasons. Her reappearance from the underworld gave her divine rulership over the autumn vineyards and wine. During her time in the underworld, the goddess serves as scribe to Ereshkigal.

Gestinana's act is the very essence of faithfulness, self-sacrifice, and unselfish loyalty to those she loves. Her motivation is one of compassion and devotion, which gives her the strength to stand firm even under the most extreme pressure.

The card of the Queen of Disks shows the goddess Gestinana. Vines and grapes in her hair signify her authority as goddess of the vineyard. Beside her is the image of a goat in a thicket, which alludes to her brother the shepherd god, as well as the earthy sign of Capricorn.

Meaning: Receptive, germinating force which carries out the process of regeneration. A mature woman (or person) who is kind, thoughtful, generous, compassionate, loving, forgiving, loyal, faithful, intuitive, responsible, dependable and truthful. She is serene, sensible, and down to earth. A nurturer who freely shares her gifts and her wealth. (*Reversed*) She may be controlling, moody, suspicious, timid, fearful, phobic, narrow-minded, indecisive, and impulsive. A spendthrift or a miser.

The Prince of Disks: Sumuqan

The god of cattle and herdsmen was *Sumuqan,* the son of Shamash. His name in Sumerian was *Sakkan,* and he was also called Amakandu and Shahhan. In the story of *Enki and the World Order,* the god of wisdom turned to the high plain, covered it with green vegetation, multiplied its cattle and made Sumuqan "king of the mountains," responsible for them. Cattle were not the only creatures under the protection of this deity—he was responsible for the care and fertility of all types of wildlife, including antelope, deer, wild sheep, goats, wild pigs, lions, wolves, jackals, bears, cheetahs, and leopards. Sumuqan was often thought of as a shepherd god. His abode was the underworld, in Ereshkigal's court.

Here we see the herdsman god Sumuqan standing on a lush, green plain. A cheetah rests at his feet and two bulls are seen behind him. Next to the god is a disk.

Meaning: An energy that is slow but steady. Unstoppable and patient force that is fertile and productive. A young man (or person) who is quiet, reserved, dependable, hard-working, steady, reliable, thoughtful, patient, uncomplaining, conventional, traditional, and practical. Slow to anger but furious and violent-tempered if roused or pushed to extremes. (*Reversed*) He may be materialistic, careless, negligent, complacent, unfocused, lazy, dull, depressed, and insensitive.

The Princess of Disks: Sala

Originally a Hurrian goddess, *Sala* became the wife of the storm god Adad in one tradition and the wife of the grain god Dagan in another. The fire god Girra is said to be her son. The name *Sala* is said by some to signify "woman." Sala is described as "the lady of the field" and, in contrast to her stormy husband Adad, "the merciful one." Sala was a goddess of grain, and her symbol was the barley stalk. She is often depicted as a nude or bare-breasted woman.

The Babylonians associated her with the constellation called the Furrow, which we now call Virgo (Latin for "maiden"). The brightest star in the constellation is Spica, which is Latin for "ear of grain." Thus Virgo was originally the Great Mother in her aspect as the grain goddess. Two thousand years ago, the season of the grain goddess would have been when the full moon was in Virgo, which would have occurred in February or early March. The growing season of Sala includes the idea of the furrow made by the plow, and the later idea of the "maiden."

Here we see Sala in a field of barley. A disk is shown at the top of the card.

Meaning: Force manifesting into physical form. Energy acquiring density. Materialization. A young woman (or person) who is loyal, purposeful, determined, diligent, responsible, persevering, generous, intelligent, sensitive, reflective,

worldly, and sensual. A good student. (*Reversed*) She may
be idle, selfish, dull-witted, wasteful, humorless, pitiful,
wasteful, and reckless.

---

1. Kramer, Samuel, *The Sumerians: Their History, Culture, and Character,*
   152.

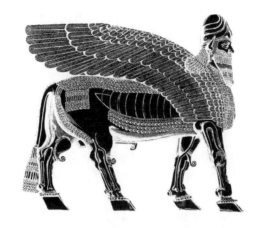

— Card Spreads —

Card Spreads

After the reader has become familiar with the cards, the next step is to shuffle the deck and lay the cards out in a particular spread to be interpreted. With time, patience, and practice anyone can use *Babylonian Tarot* for insight and divination. The following card spreads have been specifically designed for use with this deck.

The Babylonian Universe Spread

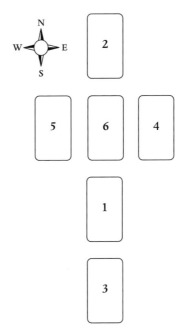

1. ***Apsu, the Freshwater ocean:*** Your subconscious mind. Deep-rooted, hidden inner strengths and/or weaknesses.

2. ***Anu, heaven:*** Celestial, spiritual, and outside strengths or influences.

3. *Arali, the Underworld:* Your fears and worries.

4. *Mashu, East Mountain:* What is coming into your life.

5. *Hubur, West River:* What is going out of your life.

6. *Babylon, the center:* Where you are at now. Potential future events.

The Rosette of the Gods Spread

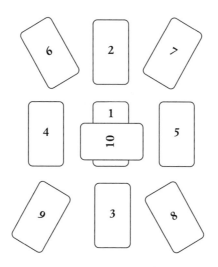

1. *Damu, the Divine Child:* You, the Querent. The present situation.

2. *Anu, the Sky Father:* Your spiritual world. (Also paternal influence.)

3. *Aruru, the Earth Mother:* Your material world. Resources. (Also maternal influence.)

4. *Ellil, god of Air:* Intellect. How you communicate and express yourself.

5. ***Ishtar, goddess of Love:*** Emotions. Your relationships and friends.

6. ***Erra, god of war:*** Opposition. What you fear. What upsets you.

7. ***Ea, god of wisdom:*** Your strength. What helps you. What you need to know.

8. ***Gestinana, loyal goddess:*** Your Family life.

9. ***Nanshe, goddess of justice:*** What you think would be fair in the situation.

10. ***Shamash, solar god of judgment:*** The final outcome or decision.

— Appendix —

Trump Correspondences

No.	Card Title	Deity/Symbol	Force	Hebrew	Path	Located Between
—	Genesis	—	—	—	—	Ain Soph & Kether
0	The Fool	Enkidu	△	א	11	Kether & Chokmah
1	The Magician	Ea	☿	ב	12	Kether & Binah
2	The High Priestess	Ishtar of Uruk	☽	ג	13	Kether & Tiphareth
3	The Empress	Aruru	♀	ד	14	Chokmah & Binah
4	The Emperor	Marduk	♈	ה	15	Chokmah & Tiphareth
5	The Hierophant	Nabu	♉	ו	16	Chokmah & Chesed
6	The Lovers	Ishtar & Tammuz	♊	ז	17	Binah & Tiphareth
7	The Chariot	Adad	♋	ח	18	Binah & Geburah
8	Strength	Gilgamesh	♌	ט	19	Chesed & Geburah
9	The Hermit	Anu	♍	י	20	Chesed & Tiphareth
10	The Wheel	Tablet of Destiny	♃	כ	21	Chesed & Netzach
11	Justice	Nanshe	♎	ל	22	Geburah & Tiphareth

Trump Correspondences

No.	Card Title	Deity/Symbol	Force	Hebrew	Path	Located Between
12	The Hanged Man	Tammuz	▽	מ	23	Geburah & Hod
13	Death	Ereshkigal	♏	נ	24	Tiphareth & Netzach
14	Temperance	Tree of Life	♐	ס	25	Tiphareth & Yesod
15	The Devil	Lamastu	♑	ע	26	Tiphareth & Hod
16	The Tower	Marduk & Tiamat	♂	פ	27	Netzach & Hod
17	The Star	Siduri	♒	צ	28	Netzach & Yesod
18	The Moon	Sin	♓	ק	29	Netzach & Malkuth
19	The Sun	Shamash	☉	ר	30	Hod & Yesod
20	Judgment	Etana & the Eagle	△ ⊕	ש	31	Hod & Malkuth
21	The Universe	Anki	♄ ▽	ת	32	Yesod & Malkuth

Pip Correspondences

Suit	No.	Title	Keyword	Element	Sephiroth	World	Decan
Wands	1	Ace of Wands	Natural Force	Fire	Kether	Atziluth	—
Wands	2	Two of Wands	Dominion	Fire	Chokmah	Atziluth	♂ in ♈, 1°–10°
Wands	3	Three of Wands	Achievement	Fire	Binah	Atziluth	☉ in ♈, 10°–20°
Wands	4	Four of Wands	Reward	Fire	Chesed	Atziluth	♀ in ♈, 20°–30°
Wands	5	Five of Wands	Conflict	Fire	Geburah	Atziluth	☿ in ♌, 1°–10°
Wands	6	Six of Wands	Victory	Fire	Tiphareth	Atziluth	♃ in ♌, 10°–20°
Wands	7	Seven of Wands	Courage	Fire	Netzach	Atziluth	♂ in ♌, 20°–30°
Wands	8	Eight of Wands	Swift Action	Fire	Hod	Atziluth	☿ in ♐, 1°–10°
Wands	9	Nine of Wands	Power	Fire	Yesod	Atziluth	☽ in ♐, 10°–20°
Wands	10	Ten of Wands	Oppression	Fire	Malkuth	Atziluth	☿ in ♐, 20°–30°
Cups	1	Ace of Cups	Fertility	Water	Kether	Briah	—
Cups	2	Two of Cups	Love	Water	Chokmah	Briah	♀ in ♋, 1°–10°
Cups	3	Three of Cups	Abundance	Water	Binah	Briah	☿ in ♋, 10°–20°
Cups	4	Four of Cups	Mixed Blessing	Water	Chesed	Briah	☽ in ♋, 20°–30°
Cups	5	Five of Cups	Loss	Water	Geburah	Briah	♂ in ♏, 1°–10°

Pip Correspondences

Suit	No.	Title	Keyword	Element	Sephiroth	World	Decan
Cups	6	Six of Cups	Pleasure	Water	Tiphareth	Briah	☉ in ♏, 10°–20°
Cups	7	Seven of Cups	Seduction	Water	Netzach	Briah	♀ in ♏, 20°–30°
Cups	8	Eight of Cups	Neglect	Water	Hod	Briah	♄ in ♓, 1°–10°
Cups	9	Nine of Cups	Contentment	Water	Yesod	Briah	♃ in ♓, 10°–20°
Cups	10	Ten of Cups	Success	Water	Malkuth	Briah	♂ in ♓, 20°–30°
Arrows	1	Ace of Arrows	Invocation	Air	Kether	Yetzirah	—
Arrows	2	Two of Arrows	Peace Restored	Air	Chokmah	Yetzirah	☽ in ♎, 1°–10°
Arrows	3	Three of Arrows	Sorrow	Air	Binah	Yetzirah	♄ in ♎, 10°–20°
Arrows	4	Four of Arrows	Rest	Air	Chesed	Yetzirah	♃ in ♎, 20°–30°
Arrows	5	Five of Arrows	Defeat	Air	Geburah	Yetzirah	♀ in ♒, 1°–10°
Arrows	6	Six of Arrows	Relief	Air	Tiphareth	Yetzirah	☿ in ♒, 10°–20°
Arrows	7	Seven of Arrows	Stealth	Air	Netzach	Yetzirah	☽ in ♒, 20°–30°
Arrows	8	Eight of Arrows	Restriction	Air	Hod	Yetzirah	♃ in ♊, 1°–10°
Arrows	9	Nine of Arrows	Cruelty	Air	Yesod	Yetzirah	♂ in ♊, 10°–20°
Arrows	10	Ten of Arrows	Ruin	Air	Malkuth	Yetzirah	☉ in ♊, 20°–30°

Pip Correspondences

Suit	No.	Title	Keyword	Element	Sephiroth	World	Decan
Disks	1	Ace of Disks	Materiality	Earth	Kether	Assiah	—
Disks	2	Two of Disks	Change	Earth	Chokmah	Assiah	♃ in ♑, 1°–10°
Disks	3	Three of Disks	Work	Earth	Binah	Assiah	♂ in ♑, 10°–20°
Disks	4	Four of Disks	Security	Earth	Chesed	Assiah	☉ in ♑, 20°–30°
Disks	5	Five of Disks	Trouble	Earth	Geburah	Assiah	☿ in ♉, 1°–10°
Disks	6	Six of Disks	Assistance	Earth	Tiphareth	Assiah	☽ in ♉, 10°–20°
Disks	7	Seven of Disks	Inertia	Earth	Netzach	Assiah	♄ in ♉, 20°–30°
Disks	8	Eight of Disks	Skill	Earth	Hod	Assiah	☉ in ♍, 1°–10°
Disks	9	Nine of Disks	Gain	Earth	Yesod	Assiah	♀ in ♍, 10°–20°
Disks	10	Ten of Disks	Completion	Earth	Malkuth	Assiah	☿ in ♍, 20°–30°

Court Card Correspondences

Suit	Title	Deity	Element	Sub-Element	World	Hebrew Letter
Wands	Kerub of Wands	Lion-headed Spirit	Fire	⊕ of △	Atziluth	מ
Wands	King of Wands	Nusku	Fire	△ of △	Atziluth	י
Wands	Queen of Wands	Aya	Fire	▽ of △	Atziluth	ה
Wands	Prince of Wands	Girra	Fire	△ of △	Atziluth	ו
Wands	Princess of Wands	Sarpanitu	Fire	▽ of △	Atziluth	ה
Cups	Kerub of Cups	Eagle-headed Spirit	Water	⊕ of ▽	Briah	מ
Cups	King of Cups	Apsu	Water	△ of ▽	Briah	י
Cups	Queen of Cups	Nammu	Water	▽ of ▽	Briah	ה
Cups	Prince of Cups	Enbilulu	Water	△ of ▽	Briah	ו
Cups	Princess of Cups	Ishara	Water	▽ of ▽	Briah	ה

Court Card Correspondences

Suit	Title	Deity	Element	Sub-Element	World	Hebrew Letter
Arrows	Kerub of Arrows	Human-headed Spirit	Air	⊕ of △	Yetzirah	מ
Arrows	King of Arrows	Ellil	Air	△ of △	Yetzirah	י
Arrows	Queen of Arrows	Ishtar of Arba'il	Air	▽ of △	Yetzirah	ה
Arrows	Prince of Arrows	Erra	Air	△ of △	Yetzirah	ו
Arrows	Princess of Arrows	Ninlil	Air	▽ of △	Yetzirah	ה
Disks	Kerub of Disks	Human-headed Bull	Earth	⊕ of ▽	Assiah	מ
Disks	King of Disks	Ninurta	Earth	△ of ▽	Assiah	י
Disks	Queen of Disks	Gestinana	Earth	▽ of ▽	Assiah	ה
Disks	Prince of Disks	Sumuqan	Earth	△ of ▽	Assiah	ו
Disks	Princess of Disks	Sala	Earth	▽ of ▽	Assiah	ה

— Bibliography —

Abusch, Tzvi. "Gilgamesh: Hero, King, God and Striving Man," *Archeological Odyssey* 3, no. 4 (July–August 2000).

Bertman, Stephan. *Handbook to Life in Ancient Mesopotamia*, New York: Facts On File, Inc., 2003.

Bienkowski, Piotr, and Alan Millard. *Dictionary of the Ancient Near East*, Philadelphia: University of Pennsylvania Press, 2000.

Black, Jeremy, and Anthony Green. *Gods, Demons and Symbols of Ancient Mesopotamia: An Illustrated Dictionary*, Austin, TX: University of Texas Press, 1992.

Bottéro, Jean. *Religion in Ancient Mesopotamia*, Chicago: University of Chicago Press, 2001.

British Museum. *The Babylonian Legends of the Creation* (The Project Gutenberg Etext *The Babylonian Legends of the Creation* by the British Museum, http://promo.net/pg, 2003).

Budge, E. A. *The Babylonian Story of the Deluge and the Epic of Gilgamesh*, Whitefish, MT: Kessinger Publishing Co., n.d. (original 1929).

Cicero, Chic and Sandra Tabatha. *The Essential Golden Dawn*, St. Paul, MN: Llewellyn Publications, 2003.

———. *The Golden Dawn Magical Tarot*, St. Paul, MN: Llewellyn Publications, 2000.

———. *The Magical Pantheons: The Golden Dawn Journal, Book IV*, St. Paul, MN: Llewellyn Publications, 1998.

———. *The New Golden Dawn Ritual Tarot*, St. Paul, MN: Llewellyn Publications, 1991.

Dalley, Stephanie, trans. *Myths from Mesopotamia: Creation, The Flood, Gilgamesh, and Others*, New York: Oxford University Press, 2000.

Douglas, Alfred. *The Tarot: The Origins, Meaning and Uses of the Cards*, Harmondsworth, UK: Penguin Books, 1972.

George, Andrew. *The Epic of Gilgamesh: The Babylonian Epic Poem and Other Texts in Akkadian and Sumerian*, Harmondsworth, UK: Penguin Classics, 1999.

Gleadow, Rupert. *The Origin of the Zodiac*, New York: Castle Books, 1968.

Gray, Eden. *The Tarot Revealed*, New York: Signet, New American Library, 1969.

Herodotus. *Histories*, Ware, UK: Wordsworth Editions Limited, 1996.

Houston, Mary G. *Ancient Egyptian, Mesopotamian & Persian Costume*, New York: Dover Publications, Inc., 2002.

Jackson, Danny P. *The Epic of Gilgamesh*, Wauconda, IL: Bolchazy-Carducci, 2000.

Jastrow, Morris. *The Civilization of Babylonia and Assyria*, Philadelphia and London: J.B. Lippincott Co., 1915.

———. *The Religion of Babylonia and Assyria*, Boston: Ginn & Company, 1898.

Jordan, Michael. *Encyclopedia of Gods*, New York: Facts On File, Inc., 1993.

King, Leonard W. *Babylonian Magic and Sorcery*, London: Luzac and Co., 1896.

———. *The Seven Tablets of Creation: Or the Babylonian and Assyrian Legends Concerning the Creation of the World and of Mankind*, London: Luzac and Co., 1902.

Kovacs, Maureen Gallery, trans. *The Epic of Gilgamesh*, Stanford, CA: Stanford University Press, 1989.

Kramer, Samuel Noah. *The Sacred Marriage Rite: Aspects of Faith, Myth, and Ritual in Ancient Sumer*, Bloomington: University of Indiana Press, 1969.

———. *The Sumerians: Their History, Culture, and Character*, Chicago: University of Chicago Press, 1963.

Lambert, W. G. *Babylonian Wisdom Literature*, Winona Lake, IN: Eisenbrauns Inc., 1996.

Langdon, Stephen: *The Epic of Gilgamesh*, Philadelphia: Philadephia University Museum, 1917.

Leick, Gwendolyn. *The Babylonians: An Introduction*, New York: Routledge, 2003.

Lenormant, Francois. *Chaldean Magic: Its Origin and Development*, Whitefish, MT: Kessinger Publishing Co., n.d. (original 1877).

Olcott, William Tyler. *Star Lore of All Ages*, New York: G. P. Putnam's Sons, The Nickerbocker Press, 1911.

Perera, Sylvia Brinton. *Descent to the Goddess, A Way of Initiation for Women*, Toronto: Inner City Books, 1981.

Pinches, Theophilus G. *The Religion of Babylonia and Assyria*, originally published by Archibald Constable & Co. Ltd., 1906. (The Project Gutenberg Etext *The Religion of Babylonia and Assyria* by Theophilus G. Pinches, http://promo.net/pg, 2000.)

Pollack, Rachel. *Seventy-Eight Degrees of Wisdom: A Book of Tarot*, London: Thorsons, 1997.

Pritchard, James. *Ancient Near Eastern Texts Relating to the Old Testament*, 3rd Edition, trans. E. A. Speiser, Princeton, NJ: Princeton University Press, 1969.

Saggs, H. W. F. *The Babylonians: A Survey of the Ancient Civilization of the Tigris–Euphrates Valley*, London: The Folio Society, 1999.

Smith, George. *The Chaldean Account of Genesis*, London: Sampson Low, Marston, Searle, and Rivington, 1876.

Spence, Lewis. *Myths and Legends of Babylonia & Assyria*, London: George G. Harrap & Co., 1916.

Thompson, R. C. *The Epic of Gilgamesh*, London: Luzac and Co. (1900?).

Van Der Toorn, Karel, Bob Becking and Van Der Horst, eds. *Dictionary of Deities and Demons in the Bible*, Grand Rapids, MI: Brill Academic Publishers and William B. Eerdmans Publishing Co., 1999.

Wolkstein, Diane, and Samuel Noah Kramer. *Inanna: Queen of Heaven and Earth*, New York: Harper & Row, 1983.

The Golden Dawn
Enochian Skrying Tarot
Your Complete System for Divination

CHIC AND SANDRA TABATHA CICERO
DECK CREATED BY BILL AND JUDI GENAW

As the most comprehensive and versatile Enochian Tarot deck ever created, *The Golden Dawn Enochian Skrying Tarot* incorporates one of the most powerful systems of magic around: Enochian magic. Its form of divination, however, has not been easy to master. This deck changes that. Beginners and adepts alike finally have an easy way to use the Enochian system as a potent stepping stone to growth in the Western esoteric tradition.

This is the only deck that contains the complete symbolism of the Watchtower squares. It unites the related energies and correspondences of each Enochian pyramid and the Tablet of Union to create the Archangelic names that rule the entire system.

0-7387-0201-3, Boxed kit includes 89 full-color cards and 6 x 9, 432-pp. book $39.95

The Essential Golden Dawn
An Introduction to High Magic

CHIC CICERO AND
SANDRA TABATHA CICERO

Is the Golden Dawn system for you? Today the Golden Dawn is one of the most sought-after and respected systems of magic in the world. Over a century old, it's considered the capstone of the Western Esoteric Tradition. Yet many of the available books on the subject are too complex or overwhelming for readers just beginning to explore alternative spiritual paths.

The Essential Golden Dawn is for those who simply want to find out what the Golden Dawn is and what it has to offer. It answers questions such as: What is Hermeticism? How does magic work? Who started the Golden Dawn? What are its philosophies and principles? It helps readers determine whether this system is for them, and then it guides them into further exploration as well as basic ritual work.

0-7387-0310-9, 336 pp., 6 x 9 $16.95

The Complete Tarot Reader
Everything You Need to Know from Start to Finish

TERESA C. MICHELSEN

Teresa Michelsen's one-of-a-kind self-study program helps students develop a long-lasting, intuitive approach to Tarot reading that works with any Tarot deck! Instead of memorizing standard card meanings and spreads, readers are encouraged to use their own life experiences and knowledge to craft a personal understanding of the cards.

Organized like a study guide, this book includes study goals, progress activities, and easy exercises for exploring the suits, court cards, major arcana, and a variety of reading techniques, including methods to work with reversals, dignities, timed readings, and large spreads. Michelson also discusses the underlying structures and patterns in the Tarot and how various cards are related to astrology, numerology, psychology, and myth. Practical aspects of Tarot reading—difficult clients, reader's block, good questions, and ethical issues—are also covered.

0-7387-0434-2, 288 pp., 7½ x 9⅛, illus.   **$15.95**

Animals Divine Tarot

LISA HUNT
FOREWORD BY KRIS WALDHERR

Ever present in art and mythology, animals have made an indelible impression on our psyche. The *Animals Divine Tarot* can help us reconnect with the natural world and tune into animal energies for a more intuitive, insightful outlook on life.

Gorgeous and graceful, Lisa Hunt's watercolor imagery showcases sacred creatures and deities from a myriad of cultures: Aztec, Incan, Indian, Japanese, African, Native American, Greek, Roman, and others. Bast, the cat-headed goddess of Egypt, proudly fulfills the High Priestess role while the adventurous coyote treads a rocky path as The Fool. Inspiring imagination and contemplation, this soulful tarot deck invites us to recognize our inner creatures and merge with our animal energies.

0-7387-0321-4, Boxed kit includes 78-card deck, black organdy bag, and 216-pp. book. **$24.95**

Tarot Shadow Work
Using the Dark Symbols to Heal

CHRISTINE JETTE

Within each of us, the unconscious holds our forbidden feelings, secret wishes, and creative urges. Over time, these "dark forces" take on a life of their own and form the shadow-a powerful force of unresolved inner conflicts and unexpressed emotions that defies our efforts to control it. The shadow becomes our inner saboteur, martyr, victim, addict, sadist, masochist, or tyrant.

Tarot Shadow Work shows you how to free yourself from the shadow's power. Through Tarot work, journaling, meditation, creative visualization, and dream work, you will bring the shadow into the light, thus regaining your rightful place as the author of your own life.

This is not a book of traditional Tarot definitions and their reversed meaning. Instead, it takes each of the 22 cards of the major arcana (the Fool through the World), and depicts its dual nature of life. *Tarot Shadow Work* is the only book that uses the Tarot exclusively for conflict resolution and healing past hurts.

1-56718-408-1, 240 pp., 6 x 9, illus.   **$12.95**

The Enochian Tarot

GERALD AND BETTY SCHUELER

The popular deck of cards known as the Tarot has been used for many centuries for divination, fortunetelling, and self-initiation through meditation. *The Enochian Tarot*, an 86-card deck, is the first to utilize the mystery and magical power inherent in Enochian Magic.

The Enochian Tarot explains in detail the meaningful correspondences behind the structure of this deck. It discusses, for example, the difference between the 22 Paths on the Qabalistic Tree of Life, on which traditional Tarot decks are based, and the 30 Aethyrs of Enochian Magick (the Enochian deck has 8 extra cards because there are 8 more Aethyrs than Paths). The book also includes tables and figures for easy comprehension of an otherwise difficult subject, as well as tips for reading the cards for fun or profit.

The unique system of Enochian Magick was revealed to John Dee, court astrologer to Queen Elizabeth I of England, and his partner Edward Kelly by the Enochian Angels who inhabit the Watchtowers and Aethyrs of the subtle regions of the universe. The authors are foremost authorities on this subject and have published a number of books that have made a fascinating magical system accessible to a wide audience.

1-56718-620-3, Boxed mini-kit (3 x 5) includes 86-card deck and 144-pp. mini-book in a slipcase   **$24.95**

The Pythagorean Tarot

JOHN OPSOPAUS
ILLUSTRATIONS BY RHO

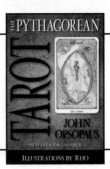

To many of us, he's the ancient Greek mathematician who developed the theorem for right triangles. But Pythagoras was also a philosopher and a magician—and, some would argue, the founder of the entire Western occult tradition.

Most ways of understanding the tarot owe a major debt to Pythagoras. Finally, a deck that focuses on Pythagorean numerology has been created. The tarot contains the usual set of 22 major arcana and 56 minor arcana cards, but with an order based on an older system. The symbolism and meanings follow the traditions of ancient Greek Pagan spirituality and philosophy, with Greek lettering, Greek and Roman deities, and a Latin motto. In addition, the author has devised two different systems using dice for selecting individual arcana.

1-56718-449-9, Boxed kit includes 78-card deck and 480-pp., 6 x 9, illus. guidebook   **$39.95**

Revelations Tarot

Zach Wong

Many feel that interpreting reversals, the upside-down cards in a tarot spread, offers additional depth and insight to readings. But reversals are not easy for those who haven't mastered this age-old divination practice.

Revelations Tarot makes it easy for beginners to use simple reversals. Each card of this exquisite deck has reversible images that allow for interpretation no matter which way the card is laid. Striking imagery-bearing a sophisticated stained glass style with illuminated colors-enliven all the major and minor arcana of this innovative, Rider-Waite-based deck. Divinatory meanings of the cards and their reversals, along with several spreads, are provided in the accompanying *Revelations Tarot Companion*.

0-7387-0607-8, Boxed kit includes 78-card deck, organdy back, and 216-pp. book **$24.95**

The Tarot Companion
An Essential Reference Guide

TRACY PORTER

While some people are so psychically gifted they can give an accurate tarot reading without any formal training, most of us need to develop our inherent intuition. The first step in doing that is to study the symbolism imbedded in the cards. This book is a complete reference to those symbols for all tarot readers, beginning through advanced.

The different symbol systems covered in this book include the following:

1. Astrology, which was central to the development of the Major Arcana.

2. Numerology which is fundamental to understanding the tarot as each card was placed in its sequence for a particular reason.

3. Cabala, which is essential if you want to progress from novice to the more advanced stages.

4. I-Ching and runes, which evolved separately from the tarot, but which can help you align harmoniously with world-wide philosophies.

5. Colors and chakras, which will help you understand the nuances in the scenes and the backgrounds.

1-56718-574-6, 264 pp., 5³⁄₁₆ x 8   **$12.95**

The Complete Book of Tarot Reversals

Mary K. Greer

The topsy-turvy world of upside-down cards.

What do you do with the "other half" of a Tarot reading: the reversed cards? Just ignore them as many people do? Tarot Reversals reveals everything you need to know for reading the most maligned and misunderstood part of a spread. These interpretations offer inner support, positive advice, and descriptions of the learning opportunities available, yet with a twist that is uniquely their own.

Enhance and deepen the quality of your consultations as you experiment with the eleven different methods of reading reversed cards. Use the author's interpretations to stimulate your own intuitive ideas. Struggle in the dark no longer.

1. The author has a strong reputation with Tarot enthusiasts

2. The first book to fully and exclusively address the interpretation of cards that appear upside-down in a Tarot spread

3. Features eleven different methods of determining reversed card meanings

4. For readers at all levels of expertise

1-56718-285-2, 6 x 9, 288 pp.   **$14.95**